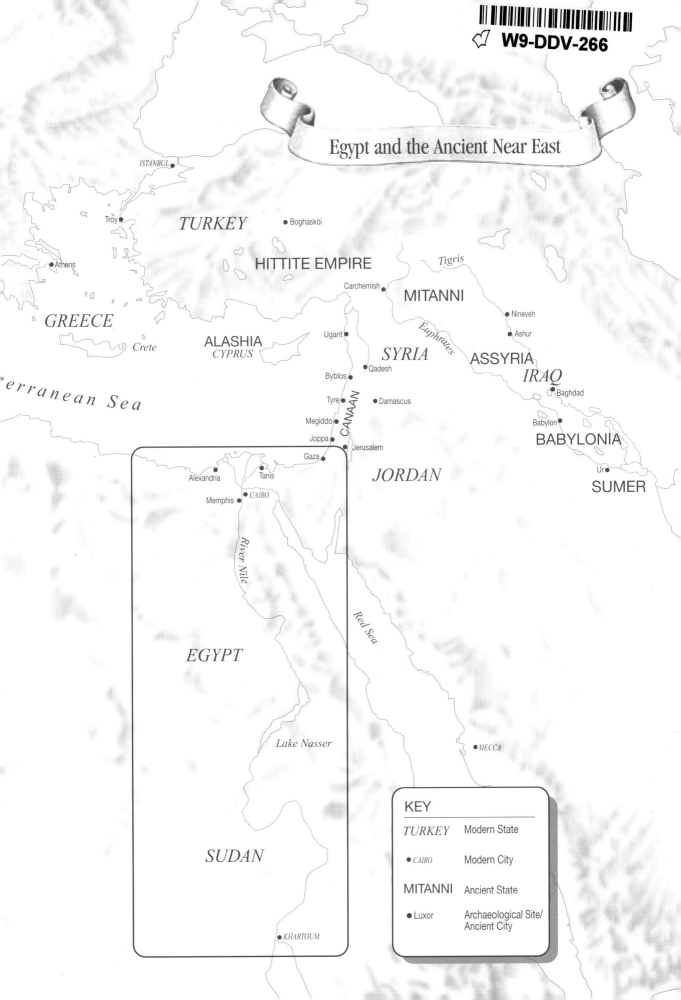

Egypt and the Ancient Near East

W9-DDV-266

ISTANBUL

Troy

TURKEY

• Boghasköi

Athens

HITTITE EMPIRE

Tigris

Carchemish

MITANNI

GREECE

Nineveh

Ashur

Crete

ALASHIA
CYPRUS

Ugarit

SYRIA

Euphrates

ASSYRIA

IRAQ

Byblos

Qadesh

Baghdad

erranean Sea

Tyre

CANAAN

• Damascus

Megiddo

Babylon

BABYLONIA

Joppa

Jerusalem

Gaza

JORDAN

Ur

Alexandria

Tanis

SUMER

Memphis

CAIRO

River Nile

EGYPT

Red Sea

Lake Nasser

• MECCA

SUDAN

KHARTOUM

KEY

TURKEY	Modern State
• *CAIRO*	Modern City
MITANNI	Ancient State
• Luxor	Archaeological Site/ Ancient City

THE
HIEROGLYPHS
OF ANCIENT EGYPT

THE HIEROGLYPHS OF ANCIENT EGYPT

AIDAN DODSON

NEW HOLLAND

First published in 2001 by New Holland Publishers (UK) Ltd
London • Cape Town • Sydney • Auckland

10 9 8 7 6 5 4 3 2 1

Garfield House, 86 Edgware Road, London W2 2EA, United Kingdom

80 McKenzie Street, Cape Town 8001, South Africa

Level 1/Unit 4, 14 Aquatic Drive, Frenchs Forest, NSW 2086, Australia

218 Lake Road, Northcote, Auckland, New Zealand

ISBN 1 85974 918 6

Publishing Manager: Jo Hemmings
Editorial: Cover(to)Cover a.t.e.
Design: Casebourne Rose Design Associates
Original Design Concept: Alan Marshall
Production: Joan Woodroffe
Cartography: William Smuts
Index: Ingrid Lock
Editorial Assistance: Jo Cleere
Editorial Direction: Yvonne McFarlane

Reproduction by Pica Digital Pte Ltd, Singapore
Printed and bound by Kyodo Printing Co (Singapore) Pte Ltd

Author's Acknowledgements
As with any written enterprise, I must thank many people. Jo Hemmings
of my publishers, who invited me to undertake the task; my dear friend
Dr Salima Ikram, of the American University in Cairo, who suggested
to her that I might wish to do so; my wife, Dyan Hilton, for reading and
commenting on the manuscript, and for 'being there'; Sheila Hilton for
her careful reading and commenting upon the final draft; and last, but
no means least, Professor John Harris and Dr Chris Eyre for first
initiating me into the language of hieroglyphs at the Universities
of Durham and Liverpool.

*Half title page: New Kingdom Papyrus of Amenemsaf; title page: the Temple
of Sethy I; opposite: Hatshepsut's obelisk at Karnak; page 6t statue of Horus
at Edfu, **c** Funerary stela of Hor, **b** scribe from Dynasty V; page 7t obelisks
at Karnak, **c** the Rosetta Stone, **b** the modern Nile*

CONTENTS

Introduction 8

CHAPTER I
THE ORIGINS OF EGYPTIAN LANGUAGE Beginnings 10
Most Ancient Egypt
The Dawn of Writing
Egyptian Names and Titles
Naming the King
That which the Sun Encircles
The Great House

CHAPTER II
THE ANCIENT EGYPTIAN LANGUAGE
The Tongue of the Pharaohs 36
The Egyptian Alphabet
The Hieroglyphic Writing System
Hand-Written Hieroglyphs and their Derivatives
Ancient Egyptian Grammar
The Coptic Period
Dates and Numbers
The Words of a Pharaoh

CHAPTER III
THREE MILLENNIA OF WRITING
Lists, Stories and Inscriptions 58
Inscriptions for the Gods
The Texts of Burial
Autobiographies
Historical Inscriptions
Chronicles
Administrative Documents
Expedition Records
Wisdom and Philosophy
Human Relationships

Stories
Texts of Magic and Medicine
The End of the Ancient Language
Hieroglyphs for the Modern Age

CHAPTER IV
THE MYSTERY OF THE HIEROGLYPHS
Hieroglyphs Eclipsed 94
Pointing the Way
Kircher's Flight of Fancy
The First Glimmers of Enlightenment

CHAPTER V
DECIPHERMENT OF THE HIEROGLYPHS
The Key is Found 104
Young and Champollion
The Rosetta Stone
The Strongman and the Queen
Exit Young
The Breakthrough
Champollion's Legacy
The Pretenders
The End of the Mystery
The End of the Beginning
The Berlin School
Modern Times

DYNASTIES AND CHRONOLOGIES 128
The Hieroglyphic Names of the Kings of Egypt
Chronology and the Kings of Ancient Egypt
Where to see hieroglyphs 136
Glossary 138
Bibliography and websites 139
Index 141
Acknowledgements 144

INTRODUCTION

I N THE HIEROGLYPHS, the ancient Egyptians produced what are perhaps the most attractive of all scripts. These images of human beings, animals, birds, insects and a vast range of inanimate objects could be carved and painted in exquisite detail, ornamenting a building or object as well as serving as a medium for imparting a particular piece of information. They also had the quality of being capable of being written in any chosen direction, even further enhancing their decorative utility.

To the outside world, they have also imparted a sense of mystery, that these images must conceal great secrets, unknowable to the uninitiated. During the long centuries that followed the death of their last ancient reader, probably early in the fifth century AD, speculations multiplied, with 'solutions' that had the sole common denominator of being more or less wrong.

The reality was that the hieroglyphs were simply a writing system, just as capable of expressing a laundry list or love poem as an impenetrably deep religious text. Alongside the superbly drawn signs on the wall of a temple or a tomb were hand-written versions that bore only a passing resemblance to their picture-prototype. From these developed further forms whose final shape was wholly divorced from the original glyph.

Hieroglyphs and their derivatives were in use for three and a half millennia, and saw many adjustments and changes during that immense period of time. However, the basic forms of the hieroglyphs were little changed, and although one can tell at a glance between texts of 3000 BC and AD 300, the signs are

the same, albeit writing an appreciably different version of the Egyptian language. From their contents, it has proved possible to reconstruct the history, society and economy of Egypt in remarkable detail. Nevertheless, the surviving written documents represent an infinitesimally small tithe of those which once existed. Thus, every new discovery may be of fundamental importance in fleshing out the picture, a small fragment perhaps revealing wholly-unknown events and persons. Such 'new' material is not just the result of archaeological excavations in Egypt. Much material, found long ago, remains unstudied in museum basements and archives, and expeditions into such dusty recesses are just as important as those to the ruins of the Nile valley.

Other 'explorations' concern the very meaning of the carved or written words. Although the basics of the Egyptian language had been re-established by the latter part of the nineteenth century, the subtleties on which the true meaning of a language depends are still the subject of active research.

This book is intended to explore some of the wide range of topics that surround Egyptian hieroglyphs. It is not about how to read them – there are many fine (and not so fine) books available designed to teach this skill. It is intended to reveal what hieroglyphs meant to the ancient inhabitants of the Nile valley, to the early scholars who struggled to understand them in the years after they went out of daily use, and to those who have over the past two centuries managed to read them once more and bring back to life the civilization to which they belonged.

CHAPTER I

THE ORIGINS OF EGYPTIAN LANGUAGE

Beginnings

I T HAS BECOME THE ULTIMATE EGYPTIAN cliché to describe Egypt as the 'gift of the Nile', a phrase coined by the Greek writer Hecetaeus (and almost universally mis-attributed to his more famous grandson, the traveller Herodotus, who visited Egypt around 450 BC). By this, Hecetaeus meant that without the river, the country and its civilization would not – could not – have existed in anything like the form that is so well known. Outside the margins of the river and the handful of oases, the country is desert. Indeed, it is as the rich strip of land along the Nile that Egypt has of old been defined.

This fertile ribbon divides into two distinct elements. In the south, the cultivable area of the river valley varies in width from nothing to a number of kilometres, beyond which it gives way to low desert that rises up rapidly to the arid plateaux of the Eastern (Arabian) and Western (Libyan) Deserts. In contrast, the Delta, beginning just north of modern Cairo, fans out in a great triangle towards the Mediterranean, with kilometre upon kilometre of flat, fertile land, criss-crossed by canals. It is completely different from the valley in both appearance and ethos.

Traditionally, the ancient Egyptian state extended from the shores of the Mediterranean to Aswan; however, at many points in its history, it reached far south into Nubia, encompassing the southern part of the present Arab Republic of Egypt (A.R.E.) and the northern part of the Democratic Republic of the Sudan. This section of the Nile, now lost below Lake Nasser, created by the building of the High Dam at Aswan, was far more barren than that

Above: *The Nile at Nag Hammadi, where lush fields give way to barren high desert. The Nile has always been Egypt's great highway, linking the Mediterranean with the heart of Africa.*

Opposite: *Ancient and Modern. The mud brick settlements along the banks of the Nile have hardly changed since remote antiquity.*

THE FOUNDATION OF EGYPT

PREDYNASTIC PERIOD
Badarian Period
5000–4000 BC
First evidence for pottery in Egypt

BLACK TOPPED RED POT
FROM ABYDOS TOMB 1730

Naqada I Period
4000–3500 BC
Development of culture

RED-LINED POT

Naqada II Period
3500–3150 BC
First major towns

SLATE
PALETTE

Naqada III Period
3150–3000 BC
First hieroglyphs

ARCHAIC PERIOD
Dynasty I
3050–2815 BC
Unification of Egypt;
royal tombs at Abydos

Dynasty II
2815–2660 BC
Royal tombs at
Saqqara

OLD KINGDOM
Dynasty III
2660–2600 BC
First pyramids

Dynasty IV
2600–2470 BC
Great pyramids
at Giza

STEP PYRAMID

PYRAMIDS AT GIZA

Above: The Temple of Khonsu at Karnak. With the exception of a few temples, such as this one, the ancient cities of Egypt are almost completely destroyed.

further north, and mainly of interest as a source of raw materials and a trade route to the far south. Communication south of Aswan was hindered by a series of cataracts, or rapids, the first just above Aswan and the sixth and last just below modern Khartoum.

Today, agriculture in Egypt is dependant upon perennial irrigation, made possible by the series of dams that have been built across the river since the beginning of the twentieth century. Before this, the growing of crops depended on the annual, natural, inundation of the Nile. In summer, rains in the Ethiopian highlands swell the river's tributaries, the Atbara and Blue Nile; today, this merely restocks Lake Nasser, but in the past it led to the flooding of the Nile valley and delta, an inundation given divine personification as the Nile river god Hapy. The water, which covered all the agricultural land, receded in October/November, leaving a rich layer of alluvium behind on the fields. Crops were planted in this fertile soil, and were ready for the harvest the following March/April, with little or no watering required in the interim.

Agriculture was the principal occupation of the Egyptian population, the majority of whom lived in small villages, dotted up and down the river. The nature of the annual inundation system meant that, apart from the period after the rising of the water – when dykes would have to be maintained to prevent the water from leaving the fields too early or flooding villages – and the seasonal sowing and harvesting of crops, work was rather easier than under modern perennial cultivation methods. Men could more easily be diverted from agricultural tasks to labour on public works, and they frequently were. The population in pharaonic times, no more than four or five million, meant that agriculture did not need to be particularly intensive to yield adequate sustenance for the people, plus a surplus which could be sold to raise the taxes needed to support the many activities of the State.

Above: *The former capital, Memphis, just south of modern Cairo, is largely covered by palm groves and modern villages.*

The population of Egypt, ranging from only two million in the New Kingdom, to perhaps five million in Roman times (and 62.5 million today) has always been mixed, comprising varied racial types, ranging from the light skin tones of the north to the dark brown seen in the far south. In addition to the indigenous population, the country was subject to considerable immigration, both peaceful and warlike, particularly into the north-east delta – as witnessed by the narratives in the Bible stories of Abraham and Joseph. By later times, Egypt was a fairly cosmopolitan society, with foreign gods worshipped in a number of centres, and men of foreign extraction holding senior government posts and military ranks.

Left: *Excavations at Tell Muqdam in 1995, which was once one of the principal cities of the area, and the seat of a petty kingdom in the eighth-century* BC. *Almost nothing can be seen above ground, apart from a few depressions and low mounds.*

The ancient cities of the Nile Delta have suffered severely from the high water table of the area, and the practice of intensive agriculture that has removed almost all surface traces. Decayed mud brick makes an excellent fertilizer, and much of the fabric of ancient settlements has been taken and recycled by farmers.

Right: The Black Pyramid of Amenemhat III (Dynasty XII), with the Bent Pyramid of Seneferu (Dynasty IV) in the distance. Both are at Dahshur, a site in the low desert directly adjacent to the lush fields that flank the Nile, where many of the greatest monuments are found. Some 900 years separate the two structures. The earlier, Seneferu's, is built of stone, the later of mud brick.

MOST ANCIENT EGYPT

People have lived in the area now called 'Egypt' since Palaeolithic (Old Stone Age) times. Then, what is now desert was covered in forests fed by numerous water courses. Many examples of stone tools survive, particularly from the Middle Palaeolithic (*c.*100,000–50,000 BC) and later, indicating a flourishing society who lived by hunting, fishing and gathering.

The dawning of the Neolithic (New Stone Age), with its adoption of agriculture, seems to have followed on from climatic changes around 7000 BC, producing what are referred to as the Fayoum A and Fayoum B cultures in Lower Egypt. Separate material cultures flourished in Upper (southern) Egypt, named after the sites where they were first identified – Badari, El-Amra, Gerza and Naqada. The first known grouping was the Badarian, which appeared just before 5000 BC. This developed into the Amratian, *c.* 4000–3500 BC (now known as Naqada I), the Gerzean, *c.* 3500–3150 BC (which is now known as Naqada II) and Naqada III (*c.* 3150–3000 BC), each distinguishable by their forms of pottery and other items. Collectively, they are usually known as the Predynastic Period, although many Egyptologists now commonly refer to Naqada III as the Protodynastic.

Below: Chapels on the water's edge at the quarry of Gebel el-Silsila, including a complete rock-cut temple (seen far right in the picture) built by the Dynasty XVIII king Horemheb. South of Thebes, sandstone becomes the dominant geological feature, taking over from the limestone of northern Egypt. Many temples were built from sandstone, much of it from Gebel el-Silsila.

By around 3300 BC, the southern Egyptian polities (bodies of people organized under a system of government) began to coalesce into a more substantial grouping, centred on the town of Hierakonpolis. It is here that we find the first known traces of large-scale ritual architecture – in effect a temple – founded perhaps as early as 3500 BC, and used for two centuries or more. After their deaths, some of those who worshipped there were

buried in a cemetery 200 metres (66 feet)to the east, in which was found the earliest known decorated tomb in Egypt, now known as Tomb 100. It was adorned with a series of painted boats, buildings, and men hunting and fighting. The existence of the unique decoration is clearly indicative of ownership at the highest elite level, and it is probable that Tomb 100 belonged to one of the early 'kings' of southern Egypt. Details remain obscure, but it seems that the following century or so saw further expansion of the southern state north-wards. As part of this, the royal cemetery moved north to the Umm el-Qaab area of Abydos, later to become one of the most sacred of all Egyptian cities of the dead. Umm el-Qaab lies at the mouth of a valley leading up into the western desert. Its early choice as a burial place may have resulted from the valley mouth being regarded as a gateway to the west, the home of the dead.

THE DAWN OF WRITING

The decoration of Tomb 100 has close affinities with the images painted on pottery of the period, in particular in its focus on boat imagery. It is with further marks on pots that progress towards writing can be seen. The vessels from the latter part of the Predynastic Period do not have the standardized painted decoration characteristic of Naqada II, but ink marks on the plain wares from the Naqada III royal tombs at Umm el-Qaab seem to be amongst the earliest manifestations of the hieroglyphic script. These ink marks form graphic depictions of various types of creature; scholars have interpreted these images as expressing the name of the tomb owner.

Above: The Ramesseum, the mortuary temple constructed for himself by Rameses II (Dynasty XIX). It stands on the desert edge at Thebes, alongside the funerary monuments of other kings of the period.

Beyond its ruins rises the Theban peak, known as El-Qurn, behind which lies the Valley of the Kings, the burial place of the kings whose temples lay in the plain. On the hills in between were cut the tomb-chapels of the officials of the state, one of the primary sources of information on the daily lives of the ancient Egyptians.

Left: The border of Egypt proper lay at Aswan, where granite outcrops produced a series of rapids, known as the First Cataract, which interrupted navigation southward. Here, on the island of Elephantine, was erected a city, the governors of which led the trading expeditions that were mounted into the African hinterland.

The most important of these large royal tombs is known as U-j. It also contained a large number of inscribed labels bearing further early forms of hieroglyphs, and numerical notations. These labels seem to give the names of various administrative entities, presumably the points of origin of the produce to which they were once attached. The precise dating of these earliest hieroglyphs is unclear, but they certainly lie somewhere within the 150 years that directly preceded the unification of Egypt, around 3050 BC.

No one can be certain what factors stimulated the development of this early script. A frequent assumption is the influence of the script developing in Mesopotamia at the time. While there is evidence for contact between this area and Egypt in Predynastic times, there are no precise dates. And while there are similarities, the Mesopotamian and Egyptian writing systems differ very considerably. In their early uses, Egyptian hieroglyphs appear as labels, both on objects, and in their incorporation into larger artistic compositions. In Mesopotamia, script was used for administration purposes, and was inscribed on clay tablets. Given these differences, the most likely link is that the idea of writing may have passed to Egypt, encouraging the local development of a wholly independent writing system.

Below: Roman Period structure from Kalabsha close to the High Dam, or Sadd el-Ali, at Aswan. Early in the twentieth century, a series of dams was built across the Nile to control its flow.

In 1960, the greatest of them was begun south of Aswan. Its construction resulted in the flooding of a 500-km (320-mile) stretch of the Nile upstream, creating Lake Nasser. Many archaeological sites were inundated, leading to a major international campaign to survey and excavate them. A number of temples, including this one, were dismantled and moved to safe locations.

Left: The rock-cut temples at Abu Simbel, the most famous of all monuments rescued when the High Dam at Aswan was built. Colossal statues adorn the facade; in the foreground hieroglyphs that spell out some of the king's names.

Above: Early Egyptian desert grave. The earliest Egyptian burial places were oval graves scooped out of the gravel of the desert edge. In some cases, the bodies buried in them became naturally dried. They were the prototypes for the artificially desiccated mummies that came later.

Previous page: The Valley of the Kings at Western Thebes, the site of most of the tombs of the kings of the New Kingdom. This view shows the tombs of Amenmesse and Rameses III on the left, Rameses VI and Tutankhamun in the centre, and Merenptah on the right.

Right: Tomb 100, at Hierakonpolis in southern Egypt, the first known decorated tomb. One wall is adorned with paintings of boats and hunters, the former reminiscent of contemporary pottery-painting; it dates to the Naqada II period.

The key event of early Egyptian history came around 3050 BC, when the whole country was finally united. While there seems now ample evidence for a southern kingdom, the existence of the northern kingdom implied by much later tradition remains questionable. The most important monument for the Unification is the Narmer Palette (*see page 21*), discovered at Hierakonpolis in 1898, and now in the Cairo Museum. Stone palettes were used for the grinding of cosmetics; decorated versions were particularly popular in late Predynastic times. In material and workmanship, the Narmer Palette follows the pattern of a series of late Predynastic slate palettes. However, it has a much more formal decorative structure, providing a prototype for many subsequent pharaonic monuments; it also incorporates early hieroglyphs. The reverse of the palette shows the Horus Narmer smiting an enemy, above whom one of the earliest known hieroglyphic groups provides a caption.

The kind of combination of images and hieroglyphics found on the Narmer Palette is close to pure picture-writing, but is also moving towards expressing narrative through abstract images. Such a combination of a pictorial scene, with signs and groups of signs making up words, is a basic feature of the whole body of documents from the earliest years of Egyptian dynastic history. The words included are not formed into sentences, yet act with the associated depictions to convey information about an event. At this point the writing system was possibly a consciously artificial one, not intended to reproduce

the contemporary spoken language directly. However, as it effectively included nouns and verbs, and was made up of signs that would become familiar in later times, the potential was there for the later full flowering of the Egyptian script and written language.

The earliest surviving texts written in an unequivocal series of sentences date from Dynasty III (2660 BC–2597 BC), the first royal house of the Old Kingdom, when temple reliefs included proper divine speeches, and private titularies within noble tombs, showing the main features of the mature script.

The evolution of the written language during the immediately preceding period is not easy to trace, particularly since the key period, the second half of Dynasty II, was disfigured by civil war, which means that the number of available sources is severely limited. Tantalizingly, the earliest connected sentence in Egyptian appears on a sealing of the reign of Seth Peribsen, directly before the outbreak of the conflict.

EGYPTIAN NAMES AND TITLES

The study of Egyptian names is a major subject in itself, and their transcription into/from other languages and scripts was the key element in the first modern decipherment of hieroglyphic texts. Names are also the ideal vehicle for new enthusiasts to begin to recognize hieroglyphs, through royal cartouches, and also private names, whose endings (🀀 or 🀁 for a male, and 🀂 for a female) provide an excellent means of impressing one's companions!

Above: Early slate palette. Images on the palettes from the last years of prehistory seem to have depicted the triumphs of chieftains, and included motifs that lie in the ancestry of hieroglyphs.

THE NARMER PALETTE DECODED

The central tableau on the reverse of the palette shows King Narmer, wearing the conical White Crown, holding an enemy by the hair, and preparing to kill him with a mace, held aloft in his other hand. Directly behind the captive is the image of a harpoon, above what is known to be the hieroglyph for a body of water. This combination clearly gives the name of the captive, or more likely the group of enemies which he represents.

However, alongside this 'simple' depiction is the complex figure above the captive. The lower part is the hieroglyph for marsh-country, to which has been added a human head; the implication is thus 'people of the marsh-country'. The hawk that has this head tethered by the nose is a synonym for the king, so that the whole group reads 'the king has captured the marsh-country', apparently commemmorating the unification of Egypt.

Poised at the top of both sides of the palette are the repeated heads of a bovine goddess. These flank a rectangular frame, with a panelled lower section, containing the images of a chisel and a catfish. Together they comprise one of the earliest known 'serekhs', a rectangular frame within which is the name of King Narmer.

REVERSE OF THE NARMER PALETTE

NAMING THE KING

THE NOMEN, OR BIRTH NAME, provides the basis for the names which modern writers use for the kings of Egypt, distinguishing rulers of the same personal name by the use of ordinals (so, 'Amenemhat II', 'Thutmose IV', etc). However, there are two basic conventions used to transcribe the names so used. One is simply to vocalize the basic transcription of the Egyptian sounds into the Latin alphabet, as described in the next chapter (*see pages 38–9*). The other is to use the form in which a given royal name has been transmitted in Greek via writers of Classical times, provided that it is recognizably based on the original Egyptian. This method has the advantage of providing a regular spelling, as the vowelling of direct transcriptions is by no means universally agreed. On the other hand, many modern Egyptologists (particularly in the USA) recoil on principal from such artificial forms as the Greek transcriptions, which in any case may be so garbled as to bear no resemblance to the Egyptian, or where no Greek equivalent is known. Thus, depending on the author being read, the same king may be referred to by a number of apparently different names. A few examples are given below; this book will use the 'Egyptian transcription' throughout for clarity.

ACADEMIC TRANSLITERATION	VOCALIZED 'EGYPTIAN TRANSCRIPTION'	VERSION USED BY GREEK WRITERS
dsr	Djoser; Djeser; Zoser	Tosothros
hw-fw	Khufu	Kheops
imn-m-h3t	Amenemhat	Ammenemes
s-n-wsrt	Senwosret; Senusert	Sesostris
iʿh-ms	Ahmose	Amosis; Amasis
imn-htp	Amenhetep; Amunhotpe; Amunhotep	Amenophis
dhwty-ms	Djehutymose; Djhutmose; Dhutmose; Thutmose	Tuthmosis
nsi-b3-nb-ddt	Nesibanebdjed	Smendes
p3-sb3-hʿ-n-niwt	Pasebakhanut	Psusennes
psmtk	Psamtik	Psammetikhos
nht-nb-f	Nakhtnebef	Nektanebo

The Kingship

At the top of the Narmer Palette is a rectangular frame, known as a serekh. It is an element found until the very end of ancient Egyptian history. Its role was to contain the first of the series of formal names by which a king was known. By the middle of Dynasty V, these names totalled five.

The name contained within the serekh was known as the *Horus name*, assumed at the time of the king's accession and representing him as the incarnation of Horus, the patron of the Egyptian monarchy. It was the primary means of designating the king during most of Dynasties I – III, but was then gradually displaced from premier position by other names within the titulary. By the New Kingdom, it was generally only found where the full list of a king's titles was being given. By that time it had become a long series of phrases, closer to a title than a simple name. For example while a typical early Horus name, Hotep-sekhemwy (that of the founder of Dynasty II) meant 'The Two Powers [the gods Horus and Seth] are content', that of Osorkon II (Dynasty XXII) was Kanakht-merymaat-sekha-su-Re-er-nesu-tawy, 'Strong Bull, beloved of Maat, whom Re has caused to appear as king of the two lands'.

The second name in the titular canon, the *Nebty name*, represented the king as protegé of Edjo and Nekhbet, respectively the great goddesses of northern and southern Egypt. Like the Horus name, it goes back to the earliest days, and was for some time the sole additional name used. At first, it may have been used to prefix the king's 'real' name, that given to him at birth. Later, however, the birth name gained its own distinct prefix, and the Nebty became a separate name. It was one of the less-used ones, and during the New Kingdom experienced the same kind of lengthening as the Horus name.

Above *Carved mace-heads depicted the activities of some of the earliest kings. Here, King 'Scorpion', who ruled just before the unification of the country, is shown cutting the first breach in the wall of an irrigation embankment.*

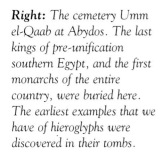

Right: *The cemetery Umm el-Qaab at Abydos. The last kings of pre-unification southern Egypt, and the first monarchs of the entire country, were buried here. The earliest examples that we have of hieroglyphs were discovered in their tombs.*

The third name in the canon, known as the *Golden Falcon name*, is the most obscure. Prefixed by the hieroglyphs for 'falcon' and 'gold', it first appears in Dynasty IV, but it is not until the Middle Kingdom that each king seems to have taken an individual example. Its significance has been much debated, and although the falcon is usually identified with Horus, this is by no means universally agreed. Likewise, although the 'gold' sign is probably to be taken at face value, an old suggestion made it a reference to the Predynastic city of Nubt (the word for 'gold' is '*nub*'), whose god was Seth. In Egyptian mythology, Seth was the enemy of Horus, and thus the whole title could be read as 'Horus [victorious] over Seth'. Although this may have been felt to be the implication in Ptolemaic times, it is now seen as being unlikely at the outset, on ideological grounds. The meaning of the title remains obscure; it may be pointed out, however, that gold was the material of the flesh of the gods, and thus the implication of the title may be 'the golden king'.

The Royal Rings

The remaining two names are the best known, and from the late Old Kingdom onwards were the principal means of identifying a king, easily recognizable by their enclosure in the oval frame, known as the cartouche. This modern name is based upon the shape's resemblance to a military gun cartridge ('cartouche' in French). It actually represents a tied rope, and is derived from the circular shen-sign (Ω), which seems to have represented the circuit of the sun, and is frequently found clasped in the talons of divine birds of prey.

The names are known by the Latin terms, *nomen* and *prenomen*. The nomen, which stands last in the canon of royal names, was the king's birth-name, sometimes embellished by an epithet such as beloved of a god. It is first found (without the cartouche) in the second half of Dynasty I, preceded by the title *nesu-bity*, 'He of the Sedge and the Bee'. It has traditionally been translated as 'King of Upper and Lower Egypt', but it now seems certain that this is wrong, the Sedge and Bee not being heraldic emblems of the north and south of Egypt, but signifying some other element of duality within the concept of kingship.

The first examples of the contemporary use of the cartouche are found during Dynasty III, although it is used retrospectively to enclose earlier kings' personal names in king lists, or other texts that need to refer to ancient rulers. By the end of Dynasty V, its prefix is changed to *si-Re* (son of the [sun god] Re). From the New Kingdom onwards, an alternative was *neb-khau* (Lord of Diadems/Appearances). At some periods, *si-Re* is written within the cartouche, in front of the actual name, but this was never usual.

Below: Monumentally sized hieroglyphs are found on the stelae that marked out the offering places adjacent to the royal tombs at Abydos. The finest gives the Horus-name of the Horus Djet, set in an enclosure with a panelled lower part. This is known as the serekh, topped with the hawk of the god Horus, patron of the king.

Left: *Label from the tomb of Den at Umm el-Qaab. It refers to his jubilee. Tomb labels are another source of early hieroglyphs.*

Prenomen and Prenomina

Unlike modern monarchs, ancient Egyptian kings of the same personal name did not use numerals to mark out individuals – William IV or Louis XIV, for example. Instead, distinction was on the basis of the whole suite of names, in particular the other cartouche name, the *prenomen*. It was preceded by one of two titles signifying dominion over the two aspects of the Egyptian realm, one of which, nesu-bity, we have already met alongside the nomen.

The prenomen is first found during Dynasty V, but was not consistently adopted by kings until the early part of Dynasty VI. It then became the standard shorthand way of designating a king until Dynasty XXVI, when the nomen took over once again. Thus, in texts where there was only space for one part of the royal titulary, a king such as Tutankhamun would be referred to by his prenomen, Nebkheperure, rather than his nomen – Tutankhamun-heqaiunshemay (Tutankhamun, ruler of the southern Heliopolis). With but a tiny handful of exceptions, the prenomen always incorporated the name of the sun-god Re. In addition, related kings might take prenomina of a basically similar form. For example, many rulers of Dynasty XVIII had names of the X-kheper(u)-Re structure; others of the Second Intermediate Period popularized a Sekhemre-X shape, X representing the variable element of the name.

In general, Egyptian kings tried to choose prenomina that had not been used before, although a number were clearly meant to recall that of an illus-

Below: *A clay tablet from Ancient Sumer (now southern Iraq) dating from around the end of the third millennium BC. The cuneiform marks on it indicate that Egypt was not the only country developing writing at that time.*

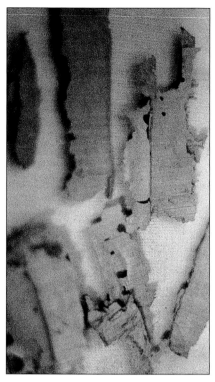

Above: Paper made from the papyrus plant was the most characteristic Egyptian writing material. The very earliest example of this comes from the middle of Dynasty I, discovered in the tomb of a nobleman at Saqqara. Unfortunately, it is blank. Although various other materials were in use, Egypt never adopted the clay tablet as a writing medium.

trious predecessor. One instance is Thutmose IV, whose 'Menkheperure' was just one letter different from Thutmose III's 'Menkheperre'. There was occasionally a repeat of an earlier usage, but normally accompanying a different nomen, and used many years after the death of the previous user. However, during the Third Intermediate Period, the system broke down, and prenomina were re-used within a few years of their last employment, but also with effectively the same nomen as before! In most cases, a minor variation in the epithets used allows historians to distinguish between two all-but-identically-named kings (e.g. Usermaetre-setpenamun Osorkon-meryamun-sibast [Osorkon II] *vs.* Usermaetre-setpenamun Osorkon-meryamun-sieset [Osorkon III]), but it can be extremely difficult. Indeed, in one such case it took some 50 years to recognize that there were two kings sharing the prenomen Hedjkheperre and the nomen Shoshenq.

Epithets

The distinction was made possible in part as a result of the study of the usage of epithets within royal names. The earliest cartouches held simple names – the penultimate king of Dynasty V had the nomen Isesi, and the prenomen Djedkare. This pattern was largely maintained until Dynasty XVIII, when kings began to add epithets to both their nomina and prenomina. In the latter case, they tended to be used only on specific occasions, not becoming an integral part of the name. For example, in a temple of the god Ptah, a king might be 'setep-en-Ptah', 'chosen of Ptah'. The same pattern is seen initially in nomina, but they become permanent parts of the cartouche by the middle of Dynasty XVIII. Amenhotep II, for example was 'netjer-heqa-On' ('divine ruler of Heliopolis'), Amenhotep III 'heqa-Waset' ('ruler of Thebes') and Amenhotep IV 'netjer-heqa-Waset' ('divine ruler of Thebes'). Almost without exception, all subsequent kings embedded one or more epithet into their nomina, the most frequent being 'mery-Amun' ('beloved of Amun'), but various other options were possible.

The prenomen first permanently incorporated an epithet under Amenhotep IV. Some of the immediately subsequent kings followed suit until a few years into the reign of Rameses II. He then added 'setep-en-Re' ('chosen of Re') to the simple Usermaetre. Epithets were then used in every ruler's prenomen until the latter few years of the Third Intermediate Period, when names reverted to their Old and Middle Kingdom simplicity.

Both nomina and prenomina remained thus (followed also by the other names within the titulary) until the last years of Egyptian independence. However, the Macedonian kings of the Ptolemaic dynasty, and their imperial Roman successors, adopted extremely elaborate cartouches that became effectively strings of epithets. In particular, the prenomen lost any trace of an easily-recognizable 'core' name. Alexander the Great had begun this by naming himself simply Setpenre-meryamun ('Chosen of Re, Beloved of Amun', both previously used purely as epithets), as did Ptolemy I. Philip

Arrhidaios and Ptolemy II used more traditional prenomina, but Ptolemy III then made the leap of using the vast prenomen Iwaennetjerwysenwy-setpenre-sekhenankhenamun ('Heir of the two sibling gods, chosen of Re, living power of Amun'); his successors emulated this length. Ptolemaic and Roman cartouches are thus easily recognized, as they usually contain double or more the number of signs of native Egyptian royal names. They also abandon the long-standing incorporation of the name of the sun god Re into the prenomen. Ptolemaic-Roman nomina are also long, with multiple epithets, commonly including 'ankhdjet-meryptah' ('living for ever, beloved of Ptah').

Roman cartouches reflect the emperor's purely nominal status as pharaoh, with major divergences from conventional formulations. Only a few of the earliest emperors, down to Domitian (AD 51–96), employed Horus, Nebty and Golden Falcon names, and not all used two cartouche names. The convention that the nomen contained the personal name was also not always obeyed, and there is often much variation between a single emperor's attestations. One set of names used by Claudius (10 BC–AD 54) had the prenomen Heqaheqau-autokrator-meryesetptah 'Ruler of Rulers, Autocrat, beloved of Isis and Ptah' and the nomen Tiberios Klaudios. In contrast, Titus (AD 39–81), eldest son of Vespasian, once used the prenomen Autokrator Titos Kaisaros, with the nomen Wespasianos-entykhu.

Below: *The king Menkaure (Dynasty IV) with the goddess Hathor and the god of the province of Thebes. Kings were considered to be gods with their own place in the Egyptian pantheon, but were often shown smaller than other deities, indicating their lesser importance.*

Father and Son

One variant on the usual patterns is found during Dynasty XIII, when a number of kings adopted what have been termed 'filiative' nomina, names that included the names of their fathers. Perhaps influenced by disputes as to legitimacy amongst certain claimants of the throne, these cartouches incorporated the names of a king's father, and sometimes even grandfather. An excellent example of the latter is Ameny-Inyotef-Amenemhat, better known as Amenemhat VI. Interestingly, his father Inyotef is not known to have been a king, but the 'Ameny' (a well known short-form of 'Amenemhat') refers back to his ruling grandfather, Amenemhat V.

These names can often place kings whose precise place in history is otherwise unknown. For example, 'Qemau-Sihornedjhiryotef' was long known, but 'Ameny-Qemau' was only identified when his ruined pyramid was discovered in 1957. The filiative nomina allowed Sihornedjhiryotef to be identified as Qemau's son, and Qemau as the probable son of Amenemhat V. This also showed that the three generations did not rule in succession, being separated by other kings, raising interesting questions about the political events of the time.

THAT WHICH THE SUN ENCIRCLES

THE CARTOUCHE IS DERIVED from a circular tied rope, known as the shen (⚲), symbolizing all that is encircled by the sun, and usually found grasped in the talons of bird-gods. In its oval form, it signified the pharaoh's universal dominion, and is the most common enclosure for royal names found on the monuments. The earliest examples date from the beginning of the Old Kingdom, and continue in use until the latter part of the Roman Period.

For much of Egyptian history, they were only used by kings, but from the later Middle Kingdom began to be used for other members of the royal family, in particular the queen. Finally, in the Graeco-Roman Period, they were occasionally used for gods' names as well.

Above: *The prenomen cartouche of Senwosret I (Kheperkare); at this period, cartouches tend to be fairly simple.*

Above: *By the late New Kingdom, prenomina had been expanded by a series of epithets, two in this case (Sethnakhte: Userkhaure-setepenre-meryamun).*

Left: *The titulary of Senwosret I: the right-hand column contains his Horus-name (in a serekh) and the prenomen; the left has the Nebty-name and nomen.*

Below: *Shoshenq IV is called Shoshenq-sibast-meryamun-netjerheqaon. Nomina had also gained numbers of epithets by the middle of Dynasty XXII.*

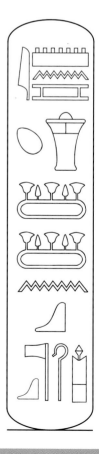

These filiative nomina are useful, because the dynasty in which they are found is particularly murky historically, and they help confirm the situation of certain monarchs. However, we know sufficiently little about the motivation behind the names that the attempt which has been made to argue that kings of the period without filiative nomina were thus usurpers, or had been nominated crown prince by a childless predecessor, cannot be proven.

Queens and their titles

The title that we usually read as 'Queen', *hemet-nesu*, means literally 'King's Wife'; queens reigning in their own right were called 'King', but usually with a feminine grammatical suffix. It is also sometimes used for 'King's Mother', who would of course frequently be the wife of a king in any case. The words for 'prince' and 'princess' were likewise simple filiatives. Two rather special titles were 'God's Father' and 'God's Mother', which could on occasion designate the parents of a king of non-royal birth. The former title, however, could hold other meanings, and has to be interpreted with care.

Above: Scene from the tomb of Prince Amenhirkopshef in the Valley of the Queens, showing the god Shu (left) and the prince's father, Rameses III.

The columns of text on the left and centre bottom read together: 'Speech by Shu, son of Re: "I give to you Upper Egypt"'. The cartouches in front of the king read: 'Lord of the Two Lands, Usermaatre-meryamun, the Lord of Appearances, Rameses-heqaon.'

Below: The priest Bakenkhonsu, who enjoyed a long career that culminated in the High Priesthood of Amun-Re, regarded as King of the Gods during the New Kingdom. The priesthood's importance was not limited to the religious sphere. The temple estates owned vast tracts of the country, and thus those who ran them had considerable temporal power.

The Officials of the State

Private individuals in Egypt were particularly keen on the use of titles. Those of high social status bore long strings of them. Since literacy was greatly prized, and limited to a small minority of society, the title of 'scribe' features highly. Literacy was the key to authority, taught by private tutors and in temple schools to, in essence, the offspring of the existing literate elite. This elite included elements of the artisan class, but most of those who could read and write in ancient Egypt can generally be classified as 'officials'.

While many titles are functional, others seem to have been intended for locating a person in the overall pecking order – 'ranking' titles. The latter were most common in the Old Kingdom, when a number of formerly functional titles seems to have become simply signifiers of status. Study of titles allows us to reconstruct much of the way in which the Egyptian state was organized, and how this changed over time. In the earliest times, the senior official under the king was the Chancellor. The translations used for many titles are purely conventional; 'Chancellor' is used for the Egyptian *sedjawty-bity*, which literally translates as 'Seal-bearer of the King' (*cf. below*). However, 'Chancellor' better expresses the implications of the title-holder's place in the state hierarchy, particularly in the early years of Egyptian history. Likewise, the Egyptian *tjaty*, which from Dynasty IV designates a new senior official, who effectively functioned as Prime Minister, is usually referred to as the 'Vizier'. During Dynasty XVIII, the post of vizier was split equally into two, with two officials, each being responsible for one half of Egypt.

This duality is also seen with other posts, although some which have been traditionally translated as denoting a 'northern' or 'southern' official, may not be. Connected with this is the point noted earlier on that the royal title *nesu-bity* may not actually mean 'King of Upper and Lower Egypt' as was formerly assumed. One issue concerns the aforementioned title, *sedjawty-bity*; this is often translated as 'Seal-Bearer of the King of Lower Egypt', but there was no corresponding *sedjawty nesu*, 'Seal-Bearer of the King of Upper Egypt'. It now seems clear that this title refers purely to 'the King' *per se*, without any geographical implications.

Many titles refer to the administration of agriculture in Egypt. The farmland of Egypt, and the surpluses it produced provided the bedrock upon which the civilization's achievements depended. Theoretically, the whole of Egypt's land belonged to the king, but in practice most of it was administered by private individuals or religious bodies. Two main areas came under the authority of religious institutions: funerary domains, where land was assigned by a dead person to provide for offerings in his tomb, and a priest to attend to it; and temples, which required land to fund offerings and the priesthood, as well as building works and maintenance. As such, the temple domains were key engines of the economy, giving a livelihood to a wide variety of agricultural, artistic, architectural and sacerdotal personnel, and producing many of the most splendid works of art of the time.

The Priesthood

The basic title that we translate as 'priest', *hem-netjer*, effectively means 'god's servant', and reminds us that the temple was regarded as the home of the god, with a 'household' like any other high-status owner-occupier. The size of that household varied greatly, depending on the deity's resources. The god of a small provincial temple might not have had any full-time priests, leading members of the local community taking it in turns to serve the god for a set period of time; in general, they held the basic priestly title, *waab*, literally 'pure'. At the other extreme, great state gods, such as Amun-Re at Thebes, had large, full-time staffs. At Karnak, the principal seat of the Amun-cult, there were no fewer than four principal priests with the title of *hem-netjer*, and numbered from 1 to 4, the first of whom we normally call the High Priest. There were also many junior members of the clergy, with such titles as the aforementioned waab and *hery-khebet* ('Lector Priest', responsible for the divine liturgy). From the New Kingdom onwards, the High Priest of Amun-Re had a female counterpart, known as the God's Wife. At first she was frequently also the Queen, but by the Third Intermediate Period she seems to have remained without an earthly spouse, and by the end of that period was the dominant figure at Thebes.

The High Priests of some of the other major gods had special traditional titles; for example, that of Re at Heliopolis was 'Greatest of Seers' (*wer-maau*), and that of Ptah of Memphis 'Greatest of Craftsmen' (*wer-kherp*), referring to Ptah's patronage of such individuals. There were, of course other local variations, reflecting the fact that Egyptian religion was not a co-ordinated whole, but a loose confederation of separate, often blatantly contradictory, doctrines and practices. Alongside the Egyptian willingness to embrace foreign cults, the religious picture in the Nile valley was far removed from the rigid cultic structures found elsewhere, in the ancient, medieval and modern world.

Above: *Paser, who held the post of vizier during the reign of Rameses II (Dynasty XIX). The vizier was the head of the pharaonic government.*

Everyday Names

By tradition, an ancient Egyptian's name was supposed to have been chosen from his or her mother's words at the time of delivery. Some do indeed seem to fit with such a mode of choice, an example being Iufeni ('He is Mine', as well as such names as Nefret ('The Beautiful'). On the other hand, many names existed that are unlikely to have been chosen in quite such a way, and reflected a considered decision – particularly when, as was common, a child was named after a grandparent. Many names associated the bearer with some deity – Ramose ('Born of Re'), Siamun ('Son of Amun'), Ptahemheb ('Ptah in Festival'), Djedmutiusankh ('Mut decrees that she live') and Hori ('The One of Horus'). Others described qualities – e.g. Qen ('The Brave'), Nakht ('The Strong'), Nedjmet ('The Sweet') – or named a profession – e.g. Pahemnetjer

THE GREAT HOUSE

THE DESIGNATION OF 'PHARAOH', applied so generally today to the ancient Egyptian kings is actually a late addition to their range of titles. The word as used today derives from the Bible, but is ultimately based on the Egyptian *per-aa*, meaning 'the Great House'. It referred to the palace, and its use to mean the ruler or government clearly parallels the modern use of 'No 10 Downing Street' to refer to the Prime Minister of Britain, 'Buckingham Palace' to Britain's monarch, 'The White House' to the President of the USA, and 'The Kremlin' to the President of Russia. It is first found as an actual royal title in late New Kingdom times, and is common by the Late Period. In Roman times during the decorative period, 'pharaoh' appears on its own, within a cartouche, in temples when the identity of the Emperor was uncertain.

Above: *Horus was the patron god of the monarchy; this colossal statue lies within his principal temple, at Edfu.*

Right: *Although a woman, the female pharaoh Hatshepsut is here shown in ordinary kingly dress, with a false beard, a kilt and a bull's tail.*

('The Priest'). Another category were 'loyalist', coupling the name of the ruling king with a favourable epithet – e.g. Menkheperre-sonbe ('Health to Menkheperre [Thutmose III]') and Rameses-nakhte ('Rameses is Strong'). A number of individuals added such a name to their birth name, this kind of dual naming being particularly common in Dynasty XXVI.

Fashions in names changed over time, and fairly few were current throughout Egyptian history. This applied both to styles of name and the gods invoked, and it is frequently possible roughly to date an individual purely on the basis of his/her name alone. For example, those of the form 'Djed-X-iuf/ius-ankh' were popular in the Third Intermediate Period, while those invoking Sobek are frequently found in the latter part of the Middle Kingdom.

Clearly, many of these names were too clumsy for day-to-day use, and short forms were common. Some took on the standing of official alternate names, and appeared on monuments alongside the 'real' name. While certain short forms were specific to their bearer, there were others that regularly went with a 'real' one. At the simplest, Amenemhat became 'Ameny', but rather further removed from their roots were 'Mahu' for Amenemheb and 'Huy' for Amenhotep. Likewise, the Biblical figure 'Moses' is almost certainly a short-ened version of a name such as 'Ramose' or 'Amunmose'.

Above: Funerary masks of two prominent figures at the court of Amenhotep III, the 'Chief of Chariots' (Cavalry General – right), Yuya, and his wife, the 'Royal Ornament' (Lady in Waiting – left), Tjuiu. Their daughter became the king's Chief Wife, the famous Queen Tiye, grandmother to Tutankhamun.

Overleaf: Procession from the temple of Rameses II at Abydos. Egyptian art included 'personifications', the representation of a place by a human figure or figures. They are usually shown as fairly fat, showing abundant food, and carrying the produce of their area.

CHAPTER II

THE ANCIENT EGYPTIAN LANGUAGE

The Tongue of the Pharaohs

Above: *The entrance pylon of the New Kingdom temple of Luxor. 'Hieroglyphs' means 'sacred writing', and the script was most at home in a religious context.*

Opposite: *Rameses I before the god Anubis in his tomb in the Valley of the Kings. The cartouches above him spell out his two principal names.*

THE EGYPTIAN LANGUAGE, the tongue of the pharaohs, is now to all intents and purposes, dead. The only place where it may be heard today, outside Egyptology classes, is in a handful of the most traditionalist of Egyptian churches. There, Coptic the very late version of Egyptian that used Greek letters, may be found in fragments of the liturgy. Coptic ceased to be an everyday tongue in the Middle Ages and is now fully understood by only a handful of scholars. The modern inhabitants of the Nile valley speak Arabic, a completely different language, originating far outside Egypt's borders.

However, there is a relationship between Arabic and ancient Egyptian. Both belong to the afro-asiatic family of languages, which covers large areas of the Levant and the northern part of Africa. Arabic belongs to the Semitic part of the group (along with Hebrew and Akkadian, the ancient language of Mesopotamia). Afro-asiatic languages have a number of features in common, including the relative importance of consonants over vowels, and the use of the same suffixes for certain parts of speech. Thus, ancient Egyptian is best explored with reference to the grammar of modern Arabic or oriental languages, rather than trying to make it work within the structural context of western languages. As we shall see, the man who deciphered hieroglyphs in modern times had purposefully immersed himself in modern oriental tongues in preparation for the task.

DEVELOPMENT OF EGYPTIAN LANGUAGE

ARCHAIC PERIOD	OLD KINGDOM	FIRST INTERMEDIATE PERIOD	SECOND INTER-MEDIATE PERIOD	NEW KINGDOM
Dynasties I–II	Dynasties III–VI	Dynasties VII–XIa	Dynasties XIV–XVII	Dynasties XVIII–XX
3050–2660 BC	2660–2200 BC	2200–2070 BC	1650–1550 BC	1550–1070 BC
Earliest script	*Old Egyptian*	*Transition to Middle Egyptian, which lasts through the Middle Kingdom, Dynasties XIb–XIII*	*Middle Egyptian*	*Middle Egyptian Transition to Late Egyptia*

STELA FROM THE TOMB OF DJET

SPHINX OF AMENEMHAT II

THIRD INTERMEDIATE PERIOD	LATE PERIOD	GRAECO-ROMAN PERIOD	COPTIC PERIOD	
Dynasties XXI–XXV	Dynasties XXVII–XXXI	Ptolemies	Romans	Byzantines
1070–664 BC	664–332 BC	332–30 BC	30 BC–AD 395	AD 395–640
Late Egyptian	*Late Egyptian*	*Demotic*	*Demotic*	*Coptic*
Demotic				*Demotic*

Middle/Late Egyption continue to be used for monumental texts into the Roman Period

FUNERARY STELA
IN COPTIC SCRIPT

THE EGYPTIAN ALPHABET

ANCIENT EGYPTIAN WAS BASED ON an alphabet of 24 consonants. Not all of these correspond directly with those found in the English alphabet, although all are present in that of such a Semitic language as Arabic. The conventional order of the signs is therefore based on that used in Semitics, as given below.

None of the signs below are true vowels. In common with modern printed Arabic and Hebrew, vowels were not written down, and had to be supplied by the reader using his or her own knowledge of the language. The sounds often transcribed today with the letters a, i and u are actually regarded as only semi-vowels, and also

HIEROGLYPH	ACADEMIC TRANSLITERATION[1]	ENGLISH EQUIVALENT	COMMENT
	3	a	
	i, j	a, i	
or	y, jj	y	
	ꜥ	a	'ayin, a gutteral sound not found in English
or	w	w, u	
	b	b	
	p	p	
	f	f	
or	m	m	
or	n	n	
	r	r	
	h	h	
	ḥ	h	An emphatic h
	ḫ	kh	
	ẖ	kh	A softer sound, perhaps closer to 'ch' or 'sh'
or	s	s	
	š	sh	
	q	q	
	k	k	
	g	g	
	t	t	
	ṯ	tj	
	d	d	
	ḏ	dj, z	

[1] As described in Chapter V, this method of transcription has been largely standard since the early part of the twentieth century. However, other conventions have existed in the past, most commonly that used by the much-reprinted Wallis Budge. The latter used various accented 'a's for the signs and 'th' 'ṯ', and 'tch' for the signs.

feature in the Arabic script, unlike the true vowels. This, of course, leads to problems when one attempts to vocalize a set of Egyptian words, either while reading in class, or producing versions of personal names that are acceptable to the non-specialist reader – twt-ʿn-imn is clearly far less palatable than Tutankhamun!

The rule generally used by Egyptologists is that if there are any clues as to the vowelling from texts in scripts that do use vowels (e.g. Akkadian, and Coptic, the very late version of Egyptian that used Greek letters), these will be used, but otherwise 'e's are added until something pronounceable is arrived at. This explains the wide variation in transcriptions of pharaohs' names found in different modern works.

Above: *A door-jamb in the tomb of Rameses VI in the Valley of the Kings. The king's prenomen and titles can clearly be seen.*

THE ENGLISH ALPHABET IN HIEROGLYPHICS

	HIEROGLYPH	TRANSLITERATION
a		ꜣ
a		i
b		b
ch		ḥ
d		d
f		f
g		g
h		h
i		i
k		k
kh		ḫ
m	or	m
n	or	n
p		p
q		q
r		r
s	or	s
sh		š
t		t
u, w	or	w
y	or	y
z		ḏ

These equivalents are only approximate.

Above and opposite: *Some hieroglyphs and their hieratic equivalents*

	Hierogl.	Louvre 3226	Lederhs.	Gurôb	Ennene	Pentoere	Harris Th.	Harris H. M.	P. Abbott	Ndm-t
22	Dyn.18	Borl. P10621, 11	c3 B.N. 202,6		Orb 9,1 il.6.	III S. 2,6 il 2,6	9,4	25,10 H. 47,2 m		
23	Dyn.18					I S. 8,11.				
26	Dyn.18		a 2,3.		Orb 12,3 il 18,4 il 19,1 19,2	I S. 2,3.	3,11	42,8 H 46,8 m	4,3 4,1 3,15	4,2
30	18 Dyn. 1	(Médum V,12)	a1,10 a1,11		N.A. 8,7 Orb 3,2	III S 1,4	5,9	26,11 H 56,63 m	4,11	4,7
31	Dyn.18		a1,2	P9785,4	N.A 12,5 Orb 12,9	III S6,4	3,9	78,8 hist		But. 4,7
32	Dyn.18		a 2,10		N.A. 5,4 14,2	III S3,10 I S6,7 III S5,3	5,1			13,10.
33 B	Dyn.18	10,2 il. 6 4,1 4,9 6,1	a1,2 il.6 il 8 il 10	P9784,10 Guroh I,1 P9785,10	N.A 7,8 N.A 10,6 N.A 52	III S.2,4 I S 3,2	10,4 10,11 7H 9,8	25,9 7H 51a6 m	2,1 6,5 1,14 5,19	9,11. 8,20. 13,4
35	Dyn.18	28,4 Borl.P10621,4	a1,1	I,1,1 P9785 16 P9784,26	N.A 4,8 Orb 18,9	I S.2,2 III S.1,10	4,9	46,4 m 25,1 H	2,4.	4 17.
B	Dasselbe Zeichen, abgekürzte Form	34,4 56,9 543		P9785,16 il 19.					5,7 il 15	5,12
36	Dyn.18				III S. 10,2					
		Thutmosis III.	Amenophis II.	Amenoph.III/IV	Menephtah, Sethos II.		Ramses IV.		Ramses IX.	21. Dynastie

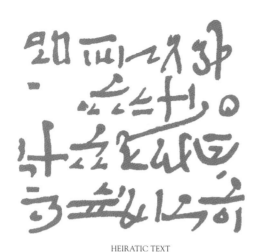

HEIRATIC TEXT

Year 27, month 4 of Peret,
day 11. The king's daughter
Nebetia, daughter of the king's
son, Siatum.

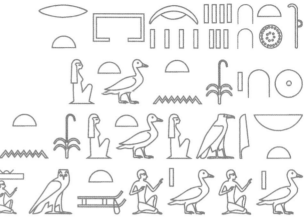

HEIROGLYPHIC TRANSCRIPTION

rnpt 27, 3bd 4 Prt
hrw 11, S3t-nsw
Nbti3 S3t
S3-nsw S3-'Itm

Above: *A hieratic text, its*
transcription and translation.
This item comes from the
label attached to the mummy
of a Dynasty XVIII princess
during her re-interment,
following robbery, in Year 27
of King Pasebkhanu I of
Dynasty XXI. To study a
hieratic text, scholars usually
convert it it into hieroglyphs.

THE HIEROGLYPHIC WRITING SYSTEM

Although almost all hieroglyphs represent an animate or inanimate object, they were not 'picture writing' in its crudest sense. Certain signs function as pictures of the things to which they refer, but the vast majority do not, or if they do, only do so indirectly. Their essential purpose is to represent the 24 letters of the Egyptian alphabet in all the combinations necessary to write the Egyptian language.

Determinatives and multitaterals

All ancient Egyptian words are made up of the sounds listed in the table and thus, in theory, any word could be written using the signs shown there. However, in practice this was not the case, and there are many hundreds of other signs which were regularly used in writing.

The first are **determinatives**. Written ancient Egyptian omitted vowels, which meant that more than one word could have exactly the same consonantal structure. An English example could be the words 'shape', 'ship', 'sheep' and 'shop'. Stripped of their vowels, they are reduced to the consonants 'SH' and 'P'. Though it might be possible to guess at which word was meant from the context or grammar, there would clearly be a problem with correctly determining the meaning. A solution might be to add a further character to hint at the meaning of the word – perhaps a picture of the item, or something which might also show what kind of word was meant. This is precisely what the Egyptians did; in our example, SH+P would be followed by 🐑 for 'sheep', ⛴ for 'ship' and ☐ (the plan of a building) for 'shop'. 'Shape' is more tricky; the noun might have a roll of papyrus ( ) to indicate an abstract, while the verb could have 𓀜, to indicate a physical action.

Opposite: *Extract from the*
text found in the pyramid of
Teti at Saqqara. The Pyramid
Texts are amongst the earliest
known examples of Egyptian
religious writings.

Unluckily for the modern (and ancient) learner, however, there was rather more to the hieroglyphic script than simply the alphabetic signs and determinatives. For alongside these were signs which could write two consonants, three consonants, or even a whole word (known as **biliteral, triliteral** and **word** signs).

BILITERAL SIGN	TRANSLITERATION	BILITERAL SIGN	TRANSLITERATION
	i r		s3
	ʿ3		sw
	wp		sn
	wn		š3
	b3		k3
	p3		tp
	pr		t3
	mi		ḏd
	mn	TRILITERAL SIGNS	
	mr		ʿnḫ
	ms		ʿḥʿ
	nb		nfr
	ḥr		nṯr
	ḥs		ḥtp
	ḫʿ		ḫpr
	ḥn		sḏm

Below: Fragment from the tomb of Sethy I, Valley of Kings. In their most elaborate forms, hieroglyphs were intricately detailed representations of the creatures or things they depicted. The falcon stands for the god Horus; the disk may represent a ball of string, and has the phonetic value 'ḥ'. The final arm, holding a flail reads 'ḥw', whose reading the preceding sign reinforces. The whole fragment thus reads 'Horus, protector (of …)'.

The line between multiliterals and word signs is a fine one; indeed, some signs can fall into both camps, depending on the context within which they are used. One way of spotting a word-sign is if it is followed by a single stroke, although this does not universally hold true. A useful guideline to classification is provided by a peculiarity in the usage of the biliterals and triliterals. These signs, although containing in themselves two or three clear consonants, are usually 'reinforced' by writing after them the alphabetic signs for their own last sounds. For example, nfr ('good/beautiful') is perfectly capable of being written with ∤ on its own – as it is in some instances, particularly where space is limited. However, usually it is written as ⌇ ; at face value, this appears to read 'nfrfr', but in fact the ⌇ and ⌇ are both what are known as 'phonetic complements'. This means that they are not read, but merely 'reinforce' the main sign. There are, however, few solid rules as to exactly how these complements are used with individual signs in individual circumstances: some triliterals occur only using one complement (e.g. ⌇, sḏm, 'to hear'), and some biliterals may be used with both their sounds written out (e.g. ⌇, b3t, 'bush').

Left: Legal document of Year 35 of King Ahmose II written on papyrus. Demotic became the script most used for administrative records during Dynasty XXVI.

Right: Palette belonging to the Royal Scribe Djhutmose. The two cavities at the top held respectively black and red pigment, mixed with water to make ink, much like water colours. The central groove held a selection of pens. Hieratic and demotic were normally written with a reed pen and ink.

HANDWRITTEN HIEROGLYPHS AND THEIR DERIVATIVES

Heiroglyphs were ideal for monumental and decorative purposes, as super-detailing with the chisel and paintbrush could be carried out if required, but they were less useful for day-to-day purposes. While the practised hand can produce a basic hiero-glyph in little more time than it takes to write a modern roman capital letter, their use would make the production of lengthy handwritten documents a laborious task. Accordingly, from early on in Egyptian history, a distinct handwritten version of the hieroglyphic script developed, known today as **hieratic**.

In its early phases, hieratic was little more than a simplification of the underlying signs, but by the Middle and New Kingdoms, it took on various distinctive attributes. The relationship between many hieratic signs and their prototypes is then far less easy to discern. The script takes on various distinctive ways of writing words, which do not mirror those found in hiero-glyphic. Hieratic script was used for a vast range of religious and domestic purposes. It was mostly used on papyri; fragments of stone or pottery, known as ostraka, were used for casual jottings.

Left: Stela from Asyut. The Greek and Roman control of Egypt after 332 BC meant that Greek rapidly came into use alongside Egyptian scripts. Many members of the Greek community adopted Egyptian mortuary customs, and hence we find many combinations of representations and language. Here, a 21-year-old named Apollonios stands before Osiris, with the Egyptian winged sun-disk above him; however, the text below is purely in Greek.

Above: *Coptic relief slab of the 6th/7th Century* AD. *It shows two strangely-shaped fishes (the symbol of Christianity) and was perhaps used as a wall decoration or grave-stone in a building erected in the area of the temple of Luxor.*

Hieratic remained the principal script for religious purposes in particular the funerary books such as the Book of the Dead — down to the latest parts of ancient Egyptian history. However, for domestic uses, the handwritten script continued to develop, and around Dynasty XXV a fully distinct variety, demotic, came into use. Although fully developed hieratic is far removed from the traditional hieroglyphs, the origins of many signs are still more or less visible. In contrast, **demotic** script is unrecognizable as a derivative of hieroglyphs, and has been described as resembling 'a set of agitated commas'.

Demotic script was primarily employed for administrative purposes, although some funerary books were prepared using it. It was designed to be written with a pen on papyrus, but there are quite a few examples of carved versions, particularly in the Ptolemaic and Roman Periods. Amongst the best known examples are certain Ptolemaic decrees which were inscribed in both hieroglyphs and demotic within temples. Some 'editions' coupled these two Egyptian versions with a Greek translation; it was one of these, the famous Rosetta Stone (*see pages 107–10*), that provided the key to the decipherment of the ancient Egyptian scripts.

The last script used to write Egyptian was **coptic**. This was based on the Greek alphabet, with the addition of certain signs from demotic to write sounds

Above: *Fragment from a wall of the tomb of Sethy I. The contrast between hieroglyphs and hieratic is shown neatly by the short ink graffito, just in front of goddess's arm on the left, which contrasts strongly with the elaborate hieroglyphs.*

Left: *Funerary stela from Sheikh Ibada (Antinoë) dating to AD 611. It shows the last phase of the ancient tongue, known as Coptic, and was particularly used for the purposes of the Egyptian church. The script used a mixture of greek letters with a few extra signs taken from demotic.*

ANCIENT EGYPTIAN GRAMMAR

A DETAILED ACCOUNT of the grammar of the various stages of the Egyptian language is beyond the scope of this book; there are many books which deal with the subject, and a number are listed in the bibliography. However, to fully understand how hieroglyphs work, one needs to understand something of the flavour of Middle Egyptian.

Sentence Structure

It is important to remember that the basic form of Egyptian is very different from that of English and most other European languages and, as already noted, is far closer to Arabic and Hebrew. The basic word order of a Middle Egyptian sentence is Verb-Subject-Object; another important feature is the frequent use of suffixes to denote pronouns.

For example,

reads rdi s mw n ḥmt.f and means 'the man gives water to his wife'. is the verb rdi, 'to give', made up of the alphabetic sign r, together with the biliteral ; s, 'man', is written with , being used as a word sign, this being indicated by the single stroke that follows it. The seated man glyph can also be used as a determinative of various male occupations, or proper names. The next signs show how the use of a hieroglyph can vary depending on context. Of the four -signs, only the last is the simple alphabetic n, the preposition 'to'. The sign actually represents water, and when three are grouped together they can act as a word-sign for 'water', reading mw. The following group comprises the biliteral ḥm, with an alphabetic t, and a seated woman as a determinative. The t is the feminine ending in Egyptian. Finally, the , f, is the third person masculine suffix pronoun, 'his'.

Tenses

In Egyptian, tenses are quite complex and do not correspond precisely to those of English. Rather than present and past, the concepts of incomplete and complete action was applied. In most cases, this does not affect the translation, but can make a difference on some occasions. Thus, the basic verb alone denotes the present; the past is indicated by the addition of an n. Thus, sḏm.f means 'he hears', and sḏm.n.f 'he heard'. In these examples, the f is the pronoun 'he'. In Egyptian, the pronoun is usually written after the verb or noun to which it refers (so we also have s3.f, 'his son', and so on). Negation is provided by placing (n) in front of the verb, although it is interesting that (e.g.) 'he does not hear' is written n sḏm.n.f and 'he did not hear' as n sḏm.f, the opposite way round from what one might have expected.

Nouns

In Middle Egyptian, nouns usually go without a definite article (an equivalent of the English a or the) although this feature is to be seen in Late Egyptian. Given that the verb to be is only used in certain circumstances, some sentences can look extremely bare. For example, 'the sun is in the sky' can appear as simply , rʿ (sun) m (in) pt (sky). Plurals (with the ending w) are indicated by either repeating a word-sign three times, or following the word with three strokes. Thus 'beauties' (nfrw) can be written either

or .

Pronouns

He, she, it, they and other pronouns are normally written as suffixes in Egyptian, although there are other types used in certain circumstances. The suffix-pronouns are as follows:

	.i	I, me, my
	.k	you, your (masculine)
	.ṯ	you, your (feminine)
	.f	he, him, his, it, its
	.s	she, her, it, its
	.n	we, us, our
	.tn	you, your
	.sn	they, them, their

Adjectives

Words describing nouns are placed after them, and have the same marks of number and gender. For example

, pr wr ('the big house' – masculine singular),

, ḥwt nfrt ('the beautiful castle' – feminine singular).

Left: Funerary stela of Hor, son of Pedimut, from the Ramesseum at Thebes. The text spells out a prayer by the deceased to the sun-god Re-Harakhty.

Below: 'Ancient' texts were sometimes 'forged' by later pharaohs. The Memphite Theology claims to be a copy of an Old Kingdom work, but study of the grammar suggests it was written in the seventh century BC.

not found in the Greek language. Its adoption accompanied the spread of Christianity through Egypt, and progressively replaced demotic in regular use. It was gradually superceded by the Arabic script and language from the seventh century AD onwards, and went out of daily use around the sixteenth century, although surviving in some church liturgy.

The version of Egyptian written with this coptic script (and known as Coptic) was the very last stage of the language, the result of three millennia of development. It was far removed from the classical forms of the language; it bears the same relationship to them as modern French does to Latin.

Part of this gulf derives from the fact that for much of Egyptian history, the written forms of the language reflected the vernacular of many centuries earlier. This was particularly the case with monumental and religious texts: some Roman period buildings were adorned with texts written in a version of the language which had gone out of daily use nearly two millennia earlier. Nevertheless, four distinct phases of linguistic development, prior to Coptic, have been identified:

Above and opposite:
Wall reliefs from the Tomb of Kaemrehu at Saqqara. Writing was the key to the administration of Egypt. These Old Kingdom scribes record the output of the workshop.

Old Egyptian Found in documents of the Old Kingdom. It has some distinctive features, but is essentially an early version of the next, classic, phase of the language.

Middle Egyptian Although probably no longer the vernacular by the Middle Kingdom, Middle Egyptian was the standard employed for almost all monuments and documents down into Dynasty XVIII. It remained in use for religious purposes until Roman times, with a slightly modified version also still used for certain literary and monumental purposes.

Late Egyptian The New Kingdom-Third Intermediate Period vernacular, elements of which begin to be found in monumental contexts at the end of Dynasty XVIII. There are changes in word order, and the addition of some foreign words, although most texts retain a heavy overlay of Middle Egyptian conventions.

Demotic The form of the language used by scribes of the Late Period. It mixes a range of idioms, running from Middle Egyptian to the Late/Ptolemaic/Roman Period vernacular.

DATES AND NUMBERS

MANY TEXTS ARE DATED, with the date being the first thing mentioned. Obviously, the era dating that places us in a particular numbered year since the supposed birth of Christ was not employed in ancient times. Instead, it was the reigning king's reign that was used to provide a time structure. An Egyptian date line might run: 'year 15, under the person of the Lord of the Two Lands, Menkheperre (Thutmose III) ...'; this corresponds approximately to 1464 BC.

The hieroglyphs for 'royal year'

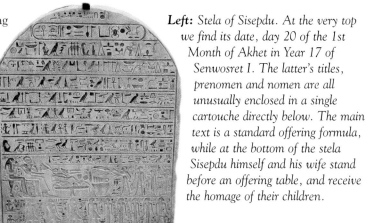

Left: *Stela of Sisepdu. At the very top we find its date, day 20 of the 1st Month of Akhet in Year 17 of Senwosret I. The latter's titles, prenomen and nomen are all unusually enclosed in a single cartouche directly below. The main text is a standard offering formula, while at the bottom of the stela Sisepdu himself and his wife stand before an offering table, and receive the homage of their children.*

are 𓆷𓊗 , reading rnpt(-sp). Up to the Old Kingdom, this term actually referred to the census of cattle that usually occurred every other year; thus, a year number 10 would actually refer to the twentieth year of the reign. For most of Egyptian history, however, it referred simply to the number of years since the king came to the throne. One slight problem is that during some periods the reign was counted from New Year's day (i.e. the first day of the first month of the official first season of the year), while during others, counting began on the king's actual date of accession. In the latter case this meant that if a pharaoh had come to the throne on (e.g.) 14 June, then 12 June Year 10 and 19 June Year 10 would be not a week apart, but 358 days.

The Egyptian year was divided into three seasons, each of which had four months of 30 days. The full 365-day year was made up by five special festival days.

The seasons were named 𓈌 , 3ḫt (Inundation) 𓏤𓉔𓇳 prt, (Winter) and 𓈙𓏠𓅱𓇳 šmw (Summer), but because the Egyptians lacked a leap-year, to take into account the 365.25-day solar year, the calendar gradually slipped until the season-names bore no relation to the agricultural cycle; only after 1,460 years did the seasons and calendar synchronize once again. A full Egyptian dateline might thus run as follows:

rnpt 12 3bd 1 prt hrw 6 ḫr ḥm n nsw-bity nbw-k3w-rꜥ (Year 12, month 1 of Winter, day 6, under the person of the Dual King Nubkaure [Amenemhat II]).

Numbers

A few numbers have been mentioned just above. The hieroglyphic script used a decimal system as follows:

𓏺	1
𓎆	10
𓍢	100
𓆼	1,000
𓂭	10,000
𓆐	100,000
𓁨	1,000,000

The signs were used in descending order; thus, 1,732,527 was written:

Below: *Tomb relief from the Mastaba of Ti at Saqqara showing farmers at work. The Egyptian year was built around the agricultural cycle, the beginning of the year nominally coinciding with the rise of the floodwaters of the Nile. There were three seasons: Inundation, Summer and Winter, each lasting 120 days.*

Above: *The Administrator of the Eastern Desert, Khnumhetep trapping birds in a clap-net, from Beni Hasan tomb 3, Dynasty XII. Nobility were frequently shown in their tombs hunting wild animals and birds, pursuing in death what they had done in life.*

Right: *In the same tomb, we see two workers picking and packing fruit in the great man's orchard.*

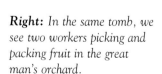

THE WORDS OF A PHAROAH

HIEROGLYPHS CAN BE READ FROM LEFT TO RIGHT, right to left, or in columns, from top to bottom. Right to left was the most usual, but this was adjusted to cope with location and decorative requirements. The orientation of the animal and bird signs indicate which way a text should be read. This stela, set up to mark the southern border of Egypt as established in Dynasty XII by Senwosret III, begins with the names and titles of the king.

Introduction to text

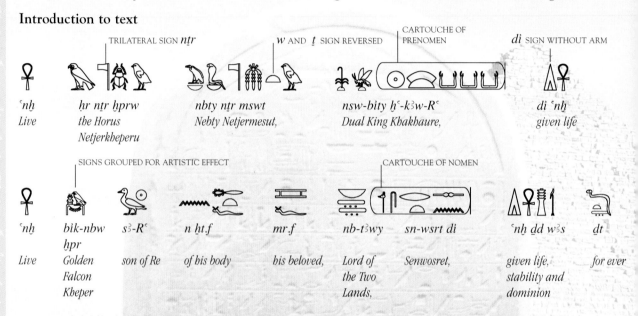

TRILATERAL SIGN *nṯr*		*w* AND *t* SIGN REVERSED	CARTOUCHE OF PRENOMEN	*dỉ* SIGN WITHOUT ARM
ˁnḫ	ḥr nṯr ḫprw	nbty nṯr mswt	nsw-bity ḫˁ-k3w-Rˁ	dỉ ˁnḫ
Live	the Horus Netjerkheperu	Nebty Netjermesut,	Dual King Khakhaure,	given life

SIGNS GROUPED FOR ARTISTIC EFFECT — CARTOUCHE OF NOMEN

ˁnḫ	bỉk-nbw ḫpr	s3-Rˁ	n ḥt.f	mr.f	nb-t3wy	sn-wsrt dỉ	ˁnḫ ḏd w3s	ḏt
Live	Golden Falcon Kheper	son of Re	of his body	his beloved,	Lord of the Two Lands,	Senwosret,	given life, stability and dominion	for ever

The signs are generally read as written, except for in the first cartouche, where the god's name, Ra, is written first, but read last; in the Golden Falcon name, where the scarab is written, for artistic impression, before the hawk; and in the second cartouche, where the first signs, *wśrt*, refer to a goddess, so are written first, but read last.

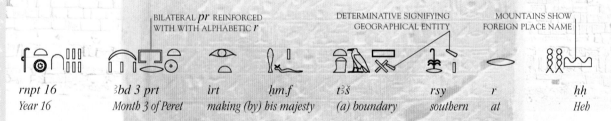

BILATERAL *pr* REINFORCED WITH WITH ALPHABETIC *r*			DETERMINATIVE SIGNIFYING GEOGRAPHICAL ENTITY	MOUNTAINS SHOW FOREIGN PLACE NAME
rnpt 16	3bd 3 prt	ỉrt	ḥm.f	t3š	rsy	r	ḥḥ
Year 16	Month 3 of Peret	making (by) his majesty		(a) boundary	southern	at	Heb

Beginning with the date, the name of the month ends with a 'sun' sign, showing that the word refers to time. 'Boundary' is spelled out with a mixture of alphabetic signs (the first, third and fourth), reinforcing the second, which is the biliteral *t3*. The last two signs are determinatives, the first of uncertain meaning, the second being a tongue of land, showing that the word is a geographical term. It is also seen in the word for 'southern', placed after its noun, as usual in Egyptian. The final sign represents mountains, and signifies a foreign place-name.

The Royal Proclamation

Where a sentence wishes to make an emphasis, it begins with a line particle i.e. derived from the verb 'to be'. The sentence is fairly simply written, except for the final word, where 'father' includes the apparent *f* sign, the snake. This is not read, being a determinative with some obscure symbolic meaning. The seated-king determinative shows that the implication of the whole group is 'royal forefathers'.

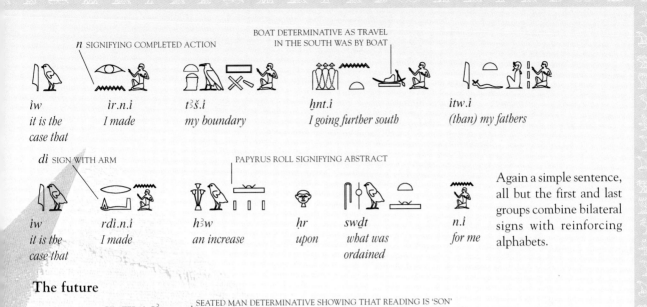

iw	$ir.n.i$	$t\exists š.i$	$hnt.i$	$itw.i$
it is the case that	I made	my boundary	I going further south	(than) my fathers

n SIGNIFYING COMPLETED ACTION

BOAT DETERMINATIVE AS TRAVEL IN THE SOUTH WAS BY BOAT

di SIGN WITH ARM

PAPYRUS ROLL SIGNIFYING ABSTRACT

iw	$rdi.n.i$	$h\exists w$	hr	$swdt$	$n.i$
it is the case that	I made	an increase	upon	what was ordained	for me

Again a simple sentence, all but the first and last groups combine bilateral signs with reinforcing alphabets.

The future

BILATERAL *s∃*

SEATED MAN DETERMINATIVE SHOWING THAT READING IS 'SON'

SEATED MAN MEANING 'I'

ir	grt	$s\exists.i$	nb	$srwdty.fy$	$t\exists š$	pn
Now,	as for	son of mine	any	who shall maintain	border	this

The third group shows how the same sign can have two usages; the first seated man determines the word 'son', the second is the masculine pronoun 'I'. The fifth group of this line is a fairly unusual form of the verb that refers to the future: if it is spelled alphabetically, determined by a bow string and the papyrus roll, the latter showing it to be an abstract idea. Both adjectives and demonstratives (e.g. 'this') are placed after their nouns.

DETERMINATIVE OF A WOMAN GIVING BIRTH

$s\exists.i$	pw	$ms.t(w).f$	n	$hm.i$
a son of mine	is (he)	who is born	of	my person

The third group shows how the passive is written in Egyptian with it inserted into the middle of the verb the *vv* is frequently left uncertain. The last group writes the first person with the sign of a hawk on a perch, in contrast to the seated man used elsewhere. This is because the king was an incarnation of the hawk god Horus and the term *ff* was a specific designation of the king himself.

NEGATIVE PREFIX

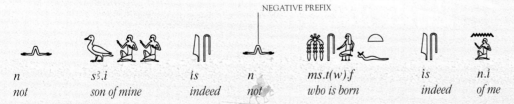

n	$s\exists.i$	is	n	$ms.t(w).f$	is	$n.i$
not	son of mine	indeed	not	who is born	indeed	of me

The same 'prospective' verb form mentioned above again appears in the third and fifth groups of hieroglyphs in this line. The latter is interesting in that the verb 'or' means 'to not', a concept alien to English language structure. A more normal negation, using the prefix *n*, is found in this final line.

CHAPTER III
THREE MILLENNIA OF WRITING

Lists, Stories and Inscriptions

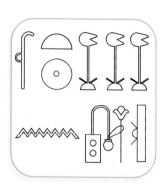

H IEROGLYPHIC SCRIPT and its direct derivatives were in use on the banks of the Nile for more than 3000 years. During this time they were employed for a wide variety of purposes, ranging from monumental inscription of the most sacred religious import to laundry-lists and tourist graffiti.

Many different materials were used as writing surfaces. The most permanent documents were carved into stone, the walls of buildings, free-standing slabs known as stelae, or the living rock. Almost all such compositions used the formal hieroglyphic script, except in very late times, when carved examples of both hieratic and demotic are to be found. Hieroglyphs were also widely used on painted surfaces, such as plastered walls and items of funerary equipment. In some cases, however, long religious texts might be written out in hieratic, using a pen, rather than a paintbrush. A particular example of this is the so-called 'Coffin Texts' of the Middle Kingdom. Most of the written decoration of the coffins of this period is properly painted in often extremely detailed hieroglyphs, but the interiors frequently feature areas in which a particular, extensive, collection of religious spells (the Coffin Texts) is added in hieratic in ink, using a reed pen. Hieratic was the script used for most everyday purposes, the principal media being ostraka (fragments of pottery or limestone), whitewashed wooden writing-boards and papyrus.

Below: Statue of Khaefre. This wonderful piece encapsulates the majesty and confidence of the Old Kingdom (Dynasties III–VI), which set most of the norms of Egyptian society.

A CHRONOLOGY OF LITERATURE

ARCHAIC PERIOD	OLD KINGDOM	FIRST INTERMEDIATE PERIOD
Dynasties I–II 3050–2660 BC *Labels; short inscriptions only*	Dynasties III–V 2660–2200 BC *Pyramid Texts First biographies*	Dynasties VII–XIa 2200–2070 BC *Decrees Biographies*

Above: *Djoser's Step Pyramid at Saqqara, the ancestor of all pyramids, signalled the birth of monumental stone architecture in Egypt. The reign of King Djoser marked a* major technological and political step forward for Egypt. *The end of years of civil war allowed rapid progress, made manifest by the beginning of the large-scale use of stone.*

MIDDLE KINGDOM	NEW KINGDOM	THIRD INTER-MEDIATE PERIOD	GRAECO-ROMAN PERIOD	
Dynasties XIb–XIII 2070–1650 BC *Coffin Texts, Stories, Wisdom texts*	Dynasties XVIII–XX 1550–1070 BC *Book of the Dead; 'Historical' texts*	Dynasties XXI–XXV 1070–664 BC *Major mythological texts: continue through Late Period, Dynasties XXVI–XXXI.*	Ptolemies 332–30 BC *Increasing Greek influence*	Romans 30 BC–AD 395

COFFIN OF MENKABU

ROMAN MUMMY MASK

Above: *The sanctuary of Sobk and Haroueris at Kom Ombo, completed by Ptolemy XII, father of the last Greek ruler of Egypt, Kleopatra VII. After the decline of the New Kingdom, the history of Egypt was marked by her increasing subjection to foreign powers. Ultimately, the country was taken over by the Greeks, and then was incorporated into the Roman Empire. Nevertheless, traditional temples to the old gods, such as this one, continued to be built.*

As we have already seen (*see page 21*) the first examples of what might be termed 'proper' Egyptian texts come in Dynasty III, coinciding with the introduction of monumental stone buildings into the archaeological record. By the foundation of Dynasty IV, around a century later, the written language was approaching maturity, with much more extensive narratives being written and, more importantly, surviving to the present day. At the same time, other manifestations of Egypt's culture were reaching their first high spots. Thus, the Old Kingdom (Dynasties III–VI) witnessed the building of the vast pyramids at Dahshur and Giza and their smaller, but brilliantly decorated, successors at Abusir and Saqqara, together with sculptures that remain amongst the masterworks of Egyptian art.

INSCRIPTIONS FOR THE GODS

Examples of the various uses to which the hieroglyphic script was put first appear in the Old Kingdom. Perhaps the most common function of hieroglyphs was to act as captions to scenes in tombs and temples. These are usually straightforward, stating what activity is being carried out, or giving snatches of the dialogue between the protagonists. In temples, these are likely to be the flowery speeches of kings and gods. However, in scenes from private tomb-chapels, which usually depict activities from daily life, in particular agricultural work, the banal chit-chat of workmen may be recorded.

PAPER FROM PLANTS

PAPYRUS IS A PAPER produced from the fibrous stem of the papyrus plant (*Cyperus papyrus*), a member of the sedge family. The long stems are sliced up, then the slices are laid across each other to form a mat, and placed in a press to produce a highly serviceable writing material. The earliest (uninscribed) example of a papyrus roll comes from the Dynasty I tomb of Hemaka at Saqqara; the material remained in use until Arab times, but then disappeared with the extinction of the papyrus plant in Egypt. However, it survived in the Sudan and elsewhere in the Mediterranean, and is now grown commercially in Egypt to provide paper for the tourist market.

Above: *Detail from the Botanical Temple within the Great Temple of Amun, Karnak. Birds roost in a papyrus thicket.*

Left: *Sphinx of Amenemhat II. After a century or more of civil war, the Middle Kingdom (Dynasties XIb–XIII) marked a restoration of central power, and a second flowering of Egypt's civilization. This sphinx had a chequered history, being inscribed both for its maker and three much later kings. Egyptian rulers often usurped their predecessors' monuments, and thus an inscribed name upon an object does not guarantee its date.*

Above: *The pylon-gateway of the temple of Luxor. It was adorned by a pair of obelisks (one of which is now in Paris) and an account of Rameses II's battle of Qadesh, in Syria.*

Above: *Scene from the Hypostyle Hall, Karnak. Hieroglyphs served as captions for a temple scene, in this case with the king making an offering to Amun-Re, King of the Gods. The hieroglyphs give the names and titles of the protagonists. The king was originally labelled as Sethy I, but his cartouches were later changed to those of his son, Rameses II.*

Below: *The tomb of Rameses VI. For many centuries, the interiors of royal tombs were simple, and largely unadorned. However, they had developed into complex series of elaborately decorated corridors and chambers by Dynasties XIX–XX.*

Temples normally featured two kinds of scenes and texts. One showed the king displaying his prowess against Egypt's enemies; the other depicted the monarch making offerings to the temple gods, accompanied by texts describing the rituals, and sometimes lengthy mythological inscriptions, including hymns and narratives relating to the relevant deities. Such texts are particularly common in temples of the Graeco-Roman Period. One example, in the temple of Horus at Edfu, gives a lengthy account of the war between Horus and his uncle, Seth; the inscription, carved in the second century BC, contains echoes of a civil war in Dynasty II, 3,000 years earlier.

The majority of temple-carvings relate to the daily cult of the god, in which the king is shown as principal officiant, although in practice a high priest would have taken his place. From these, it is possible to reconstruct much of the 'daily life' of a god in his temple – dressed and fed regularly, and carried in procession on great feast-days.

Above: *Scene from the funerary chapel of the Vizier Ramose, who flourished in the reign of Amenhotep III. It shows a nobleman's funeral, with servants carrying his possessions and a crowd of professional female mourners. Once again, the hieroglyphs provide captions to the events.*

Left: *The stela of Sennefer of Dynasty XVIII. The focal point of a chapel was its stela – indeed, for middle class individuals, their chapel may have been no more than a shelter for the stela. This usually featured the deceased in front of a table of offerings, sometimes accompanied by members of their family; the belief was that by being depicted, everything would magically be supplied to the deceased in the next world.*

THE TEXTS OF BURIAL

ALONGSIDE THOSE from the temples of the gods, texts from funerary contexts are amongst our most numerous survivals of Egyptian texts. Ideally, an Egyptian tomb comprised an above-ground offering-place and a subterranean burial chamber. The former range from a bare stela to complexes of rooms, either built into the core of a mastaba (bench-shaped tomb), or carved into a rock escarpment. Culminating in the stela, sometimes in the form of a 'false door', that served as the point of interface between this world and the next, these chapels were decorated with a wide range of scenes showing the agricultural and industrial life of the country. The stela and these scenes also bore texts in hieroglyphs, that act either as direct captions on the activities depicted, or supplying magic formulae to ensure the safe passage to, and existence in, the world beyond.

These beautifully decorated chapels, and their royal equivalents, the temple-complexes that stood before the pyramids, formed only part of the whole magical machine that was the Egyptian tomb. Far below ground was the burial chamber in which the embalmed body was to sleep out eternity. In only a few cases was this room decorated, usually with lists of offerings to sustain the dead. Late in the Old Kingdom, such lists begin to appear inside the rectangular wooden coffins that housed the body. In addition, coffins bore the earliest versions of a standard offering formula that was to become ubiquitous in Egyptian funerary contexts. This is the ḥtp di nsw, which magically provided the dead with eternal sustenance. Found throughout Egyptian history, it has a number of variants, but a typical example runs as follows:

'Royal offering to [the god] Osiris … that he may give offerings consisting of bread and beer, oxen and fowl, alabaster and clothing, all things good and pure on which a god lives, to the spirit of the deceased NAME'.

During the Middle Kingdom, more extensive funerary inscriptions begin to be found, beginning with the 'Coffin Texts', written on the interiors of wooden coffins and designed to aid the dead person's journey into the next world. This was envisaged as being to the west of the world of the living, and to reach it the dead had to endure many dangers. By the time of the New Kingdom, a complete guidebook to the journey had been prepared. This was referred to as the 'Book of Coming Forth by Day', better known today as the 'Book of the Dead'. It was usually inscribed on an illustrated papyrus

Top: *Thutmose IV offered the sign of life by the goddess of the West. The scene forms part of the extensive decoration of the king's tomb in the Valley of the Kings, where the time-hallowed pyramid was discarded in favour of concealment.*

Below: *Coffin of Pasherhorawesheb (Dynasty XXII), covered with divine images and hieroglyphs. The latter spelled out the magic formulae that ensured that the dead would go safely and well-nourished into the afterlife.*

Right: *The pyramid of Khaefre at Giza. Funerary chapels could either be cut in the rock escarpment, built into a bench-shaped structure known as a mastaba, or be completely free standing. The first two types can be seen here, on the south-east of the pyramid. During the Old and Middle Kingdoms, kings differed from their subjects in being buried under such great monuments. The remains of the pyramid's chapel may be seen against its east face.*

roll, but was also found on coffins and the walls of the tomb. It led the dead through the journey west, giving the correct response to those who guarded the gates along the way, and culminated in the deceased's trial before Osiris, King of the Dead.

Only those who had led a good life would be allowed into the world of eternity. The heart was regarded as the seat of memory and intelligence, and to test the dead person it was weighed against a feather – the hieroglyphic symbol of Maat, goddess of truth. If the scales balanced, all was well; if not, the heart was thrown to a monster, which ate it and condemned the soul to wander for eternity. But this would never happen: the illustrations in the Book of the Dead showed success, and according to Egyptian belief, if something was shown happening, by magic it did happen. This idea lies behind many images in both tombs and temples, guaranteeing continuity for ever. The written word had similar importance: as long as a person's name survived in writing, they too survived. To be utterly forgotten was a person's real death.

During the New Kingdom and later, many other funerary 'books' grew up, with different themes, but still with the intention of easing the transition between the two worlds. Most books first appeared in the tombs of the kings, and only later spread to their subjects at all levels of society.

Left: *New Kingdom papyrus of Amenemsaf. From the New Kingdom onwards, the mummy was usually equipped with an illustrated papyrus roll known as the Book of the Dead. This was a 'guidebook' for reaching the next world, normally written in hieratic. This detail shows four guardians of the dead, known as the Four Sons of Horus, from the right Imseti, Hapy, Duamutef and Qebehsenuef.*

Demetrios

*Above: Thutmose III.
During the New Kingdom
(Dynasties XVIII–XX),
Egypt became a world power.
Under Thutmose III, her
empire and collection of
satellite states extended from
northern Syria to the heart of
the Sudan.*

*Previous pages: Wall
bearing the autobiography of
Ahmose-si-Ibana at El-Kab.
It recounts his role in the
wars of liberation at the
beginning of the New
Kingdom, in which the
Palestinian Hyksos kings
were expelled from Egypt.*

AUTOBIOGRAPHIES

Besides material relating to the afterlife, burial-places also contained some of the earliest lengthy secular compositions. These are the autobiographies sometimes included by officials in their tomb-chapels. Their primary purpose is to glorify the author, particularly from the point of view of emphasizing his closeness to the king, the lynchpin of Egyptian society. In spite of this less-than-objective approach, useful factual material can often be gleaned. One of the most important of the earliest such compositions, that of Uni, from Abydos, speaks tantalizingly of his having presided over the trial of one of the wives of King Pepy I (Dynasty VI). However, nothing is said of the nature of the charges, nor the outcome, so that we can only speculate on what dynastic intrigues may have lain behind Uni's bland statements.

Some of the most fascinating texts of the Old Kingdom are the autobiographies of the governors of the southern city of Aswan. Amongst their duties were the conduct of trading expeditions into eastern and central Africa. In the text of Harkhuf, we read of a dancing dwarf being acquired somewhere in the south, the news of whom delighted his young king, Pepy II. The king's letter is quoted verbatim by Harkhuf, emphasizing his intimacy with his monarch. Yet another deals with a mission by Sabni, to recover the body of his father Mekhu, killed by bandits while on an expedition into the Eastern Desert to build a ship for a voyage down the Red Sea coast.

Autobiographies are found throughout Egyptian history. One, from the Middle Kingdom, gives us one of our most comprehensive accounts of the kind of 'passion play' that formed part of some religious festivals. Written by Ikhernofret, and found on a stela from his tomb, it gives an account of the annual festival of Osiris at Abydos. In it, the story of the life, death, resurrection and vindication of the god was re-enacted, with Ikhernofret playing important parts:

[Ikhernofret has been sent to Abydos by King Senwosret III to oversee the festival, and also renew the god's cult-image]:

I did everything that His Person commanded, putting into effect my lord's command for his father, Osiris, Lord of Abydos, great of power, who is in the Thinite nome. I acted as beloved son of Osiris. I embellished his great barque of eternity; I made for it a shrine which displays the beauties of Khentyamentiu, in gold, silver, lapis-lazuli, bronze and wood. I fashioned the gods in his train. I made their shrines anew. I caused the temple-priesthood to do their duties, I caused them to know the custom of every day, the festival of the Head-of-the-Year. I controlled work on the neshmet-barque; I fashioned the shrine and adorned the breast of the Lord of Abydos with lapis-lazuli and turquoise, electrum and every precious stone, as an adornment of the divine limbs. I changed the clothes of the god at his appearance, in the office of Master of Secrets and in my job as sem-priest. I was clean of arm in adoring the god, a sem clean of fingers.

I organized the going-forth of Wepwawet when he proceeded to avenge his father; I drove-away the rebels from the neshmet-barque; I overthrew the enemies of

Osiris; I celebrated the great going-forth. I followed the god at his going, and caused the ship to sail, Thoth steering the sailing. I equipped the barque with a chapel and affixed (Osiris)'s beautiful adornments when he proceeded to the district of Peqer. I cleared the ways of the god to his tomb before Peqer. I avenged Wennefer that day of the great fight; I overthrew all his enemies upon the sandbanks of Nedyt: I caused him to proceed into the great barque. It raised up his beauties, I making glad the people/tomb-owners of the Eastern Desert, creating joy amongst the people/tomb-owners of the Western Desert; they saw the beauties of the god's barque when it touched land at Abydos, when it brought Osiris-Khentyamentiu to his palace; I followed the god to his house, I carried out his purification and extended his seat and solved the problems of his residence [... and amongst] his entourage.

Works of Faction?

Another autobiography of this general period, now lost, may have formed the basis for the 'Story of Sinuhe', one of the classics of Egyptian literature. The exiled Sinuhe, a courtier of Amenemhat I, wanders the desert, is befriended by Bedouins, has many adventures, is finally pardoned when a new king, Sesostris I, comes to the throne, and returns to his beloved homeland. In its vivid detail and general 'feel' it clearly diverges from standard tomb autobiographies, yet it follows their basic structure and is either a pure romance using the traditional autobiography as a literary device, or Sinuhe's genuine tomb inscription greatly elaborated – either as a work of 'faction', or a genuine narrative from which a tomb inscription might have been edited down.

A similar example, from the reign of Thutmose III (Dynasty XVIII), describes the capture of the Palestinian town of Joppa by General Djehuty, whose tomb (now lost) seems to have been at Saqqara. His stratagem of smuggling his soldiers into the city, hidden in baskets carried by porters, survives in a folk-tale, but is probably based upon an original tomb inscription.

Above: *The dramatically-located tombs of Mekhu and Sabni at Aswan. Biographical inscriptions in private tombs are often banal, but a few are of considerable interest and this one contains the account of how Sabni journeyed into the Eastern Desert to retrieve the body of his dead father and punish his murderers.*

Below: *Abydos, the scene of the 'passion play' described in Ikhernofret's autobiography. The great brick mortuary enclosure of Khasekhemwy (Dynasty II), stands above the wadi in which most of the action occurred.*

Soldiers' Tales

Warriors' autobiographies from the early years of Dynasty XVIII provide much useful detail. In particular, texts in the tombs of an army officer, Ahmose-Pennekhbet, and a naval officer, Ahmose-si-Ibana, at El-Kab relate to their service in the wars of Kamose and Ahmose I that liberated northern Egypt from Palestinian rule. General Amenemhab, in his tomb at Thebes, provides details of incidents from the campaigns of Thutmose III, including one when he saved the king from a charging elephant while out hunting in north Syria.

Such informative autobiographies become less common in later times, most examples being more concerned with the offices held by the author, and how high he stood in the favour of the king and the gods. Their historical importance is often incidental, for example where the order of kings is mentioned. Similarly, officials with a royal ancestor may trace their line of descent back far enough to inform us of the names of some otherwise unknown kings and queens. One important exception is the inscription on a statue of one Udjahorresnet (now in the Vatican Museum), whose owner began his career at the end of Dynasty XXVI, and whose tomb was found at Abusir in 1980. He subsequently served the Persian kings who invaded Egypt in 525 BC, was responsible for the formulation of Egyptian titulary for the Persian ruler Kambyses (d. 522 BC) and undertook various activities relating to temple administration for his foreign masters.

Below: *Scene from the first pylon of Rameses III's mortuary temple at Medinet Habu. Rameses III smites his enemies before the god Amun. They are held together by their hair, while the king raises his mace above his head. The king's cartouches are particularly deeply carved, perhaps as a defence against those who might wish to usurp the relief in the future!*

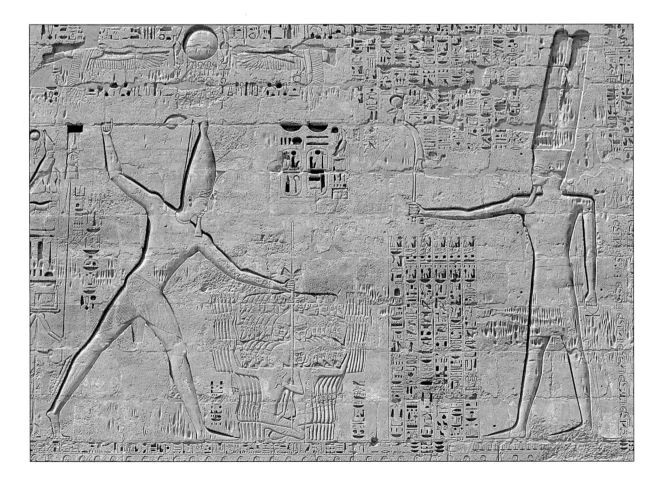

Above: *Fight scene from a tomb at Saqqara. A number of Old Kingdom tombs are decorated with scenes of boatmen carrying out mock battles, presumably for the entertainment of the resident of the tomb.*

Left: *A model army of Egyptian spearmen found in the tomb of Mesehti, a Governor of Asyut during Dynasty XI. The tomb also contained a troop of Nubian soldiers. The Governors of the nomes (provinces) of Middle Egypt were heavily involved in the civil wars that waged during the First Intermediate Period.*

HISTORICAL INSCRIPTIONS

Above: The tomb of the nobleman Rekhmire at Luxor. A procession of people bring apes, ivory and leopards, possible tributes from Egypt's lesser neighbours.

Below: Thutmose III smiting his enemies, from the temple of Amun-Re at Karnak. All Egyptian 'historical' texts had a propaganda role, and the intention here was to show the king's dominion over both Egypt and the outside world.

Lengthy royal 'historical' texts seldom survive from the early periods of Egyptian history. The term 'historical' is used advisedly, since it is important to understand that kings did not leave records of their deeds as records for posterity. Rather, monarchs commissioned texts that demonstrated how they had fulfilled the cosmic role of the king: to maintain cosmic order, defeat Egypt's enemies and provide for the cult of the gods, to name but a few of the more important royal tasks. These inscriptions often described a king's activities as an illustration of how he carried out his role, and are thus often labelled as 'historical' documents; nevertheless, they have an explicit propagandistic purpose, and accordingly must be used with great care.

One particular cautionary tale underlines this point. In the mortuary temple of Pepy II of Dynasty VI at Saqqara there is a relief of the king smiting a Libyan chieftain, while the latter's family look on. The chief and his family are all named, apparently indicating that the scene records a genuine campaign by King Pepy. However, the same scene occurs in the earlier Dynasty V temple of Sahure at Abusir – including the same names for the chief and his family. Not only this, but nearly 2,000 years later, in Dynasty XXV, King Taharqa is shown at Karnak, smiting the self-same chief, while the very same members of his family look on.

The largest body of 'historical' texts comes from the New Kingdom, when the kings of Dynasty XVIII extended Egyptian overlordship into the heart of the Sudan, and as far as the Euphrates in Syria. Many were set up in the gigantic temple of Amun-Re, King of the Gods, at Karnak, either on the walls of the temple, or on free-standing round-topped stelae. Among the most informative are those of Thutmose III, under whom the Egyptian 'Empire' reached its greatest extent. His inscriptions are less smothered in the elaborate rhetorical flourishes that frequently hinder the understanding of other examples, and they allow us to trace the progress of his military campaigns in some detail. Nevertheless, poetry was

used within one of his stelae from Karnak. The text is couched in the form of a speech to the king by Amun-Re, and after a dozen lines of plain prose the next ten lines take a clear metrical form; four of these illustrate the pattern:

> I have come that I may cause you to trample the chiefs of the Lebanon when I spread them under your feet throughout their lands;
> I cause them to see Your Majesty as lord of sunshine as you shine in their faces in my likeness.
> I have come that I may cause you to trample those of Asia, when you smite the heads of the Asiatics of Palestine;
> I cause them to see Your Majesty equipped with your ornaments as you brandish weapons to fight upon the chariot ....

Extensive texts survive relating to the campaigns of Rameses II (Dynasty XIX), in particular that which culminated in the Battle of Qadesh (c.1285 BC) against the Hittites in Syria. Two basic versions of the narrative exist, one couched in a 'poetic' form, and they can be found on the walls of at least five temples, and on papyrus. Although the battle nearly ended in disaster for the Egyptians, the inscriptions' purpose is made clear by the superhuman strength and skill attributed to the king, who is credited with single-handedly turning the tide of the battle.

Amongst later royal texts, the stela of the Nubian king Piye (Dynasty XXV), from Napata in the Sudan, stands out. It relates the conquest of Egypt by the ruler of Nubia, reversing the trend of history, which had normally seen the southern country subjugated by Egypt. Its inhabitants were not well regarded by their northern neighbours, a stela of Senwosret III (Dynasty XII) from Semna (see also pages 56–7), then the Egypto-Nubian border, and now in Berlin, states that a Nubian

> .... listens, to fall at a word:
> To answer him is to make him retreat;
> Attack him: he will turn his back;
> Retreat: he will start attacking.
> They are not people worthy of respect,
> They are wretches, craven-hearted!
> My person has seen it: it is not a lie!

However, during Dynasties XXII–XXIII, Egypt had gradually fallen into a number of separate petty polities, the southernmost of which, centred on Thebes, had come under the effective control of the kings of Nubia. In response to the expansionist plans of one of the rulers of the far north (Tefnakhte, of Dynasty XXIV), Piye had marched into Lower Egypt, and succeeded in forcing the various local potentates, including four 'pharaohs' to accept him as paramount ruler. The language used in the stela is unusually straightforward, and allows us to follow the events of this historic event in more detail than is often possible.

Above: Pylon VIII of the Karnak temple, dating to Dynasty XVIII. The pylon gateways of the principal temples were prime sites for propagandist inscriptions.

Below: The 'poetic' stela of Thutmose III, from Karnak. Most 'historical' inscriptions were to be found on large stelae, placed around the main temples.

CHRONICLES

Above: A basalt slab recycled as the lid of the sarcophagus of Ankhnespepy a late Dynasty VI queen. It had once been covered with a chronicle, listing accounts of each year of the reigns of earlier kings.

Below: The Turin Canon of Kings. Although it is the most comprehensive chronicle document known to date, severe damage has left it with many frustrating gaps.

An exception to such highly partial 'historical' texts are a small group of items which, at first sight at least, may represent an attempt at a basic recording of historical data. The best known is a slab of basalt, now known as the Palermo Stone because it is in the museum at Palermo. Now damaged, when complete, it appears to have provided a year-by-year chronicle of Egypt, from the unification of Egypt down to the middle of Dynasty V, together with a list of the preceding rulers of the separate Upper and Lower Egyptian polities. Unfortunately, the vast majority is missing, while a second copy, mainly in Cairo, is even less complete. A document of similar format was identified in the 1990s, which seems to have carried on the chronicle into Dynasty VI. Regrettably, it had been re-used as a sarcophagus lid at the very end of that dynasty, and almost all the text has been worn away.

A much later document of a similar kind is the papyrus now in the Turin Egyptian Museum. Written early in Dynasty XIX, it contains a complete list of kings, from the rule of the gods onwards, with each monarch's reign-length recorded, down to the nearest day. Unfortunately, it has been very severely damaged, and only a small proportion of its priceless information is preserved.

Often bracketed with these documents are the so-called 'king-lists', which were found in the temples of Karnak and Abydos, and a tomb at Saqqara. Dating from Dynasty XVIII and XIX, they are actually lists of deceased kings to whom a prayer is offered. On all but one of these monuments, the kings are listed in chronological order, but this is clearly for the convenience of the scribe who laid out the texts. The lists have also been edited to fit the available wall space, with obscure or proscribed kings omitted. The 'historical' value of these lists is thus incidental – although very real in establishing the order of certain obscure rulers.

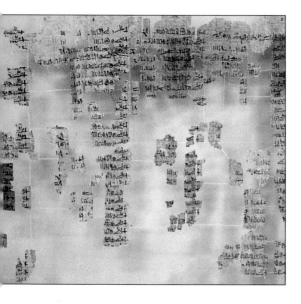

Left: *The temple of Sethy I, one of the best preserved in Egypt. Its king list lies in one of the rear corridors of the building.*

Above: *Sethy I and his son, Crown Prince Rameses (later II), seen to the left of the list in Sethy's temple. Rameses reads a prayer from a scroll, which is for the benefit of the long list of kings whose cartouches are carved in front of him. Although generally accurate, many kings are omitted. Some, including the whole of Dynasties XIII–XVII, seem to have been missed out for reasons of space, while others, such as Tutankhamun, had been wiped from history for political reasons.*

Opposite: *The temple of Sethy I at Abydos. A list of recipients of temple offerings found here conveniently places ancient kings in their historical order.*

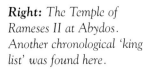

Right: *The Temple of Rameses II at Abydos. Another chronological 'king list' was found here.*

ADMINISTRATIVE DOCUMENTS

Above: The pyramid of Senwosret II at Lahun. It was serviced by Kahun, a 'workmen's settlement' set up in Dynasty XII. Kahun is one of our best sources for administrative documents.

Below: Kahun lay in a now-desolate area alongside the vanished valley temple, 1.6 km (1 mile) to the east. Many papyrus documents were found in and adjacent to the town, and are now in Berlin and London.

Other 'historical' written material includes surviving administrative documents. A wide range exists, generally written on papyrus or ostraka, in cursive forms of the hieroglyphic script. The workmen of the Theban village of Deir el-Medina, who built the tombs of the pharaohs, have left behind material that both explains the way in which work was organized, and illuminates the lives of the workers themselves and their families. The joys and tribulations of family life are well illustrated, including some choice scandals and even acts of homicide. In addition, the records include those of the first known strike and sit-in.

The work journals from Deir el-Medina are also useful in reconstructing the chronology of Dynasties XIX–XX, because almost every year of every king is recorded. From a 'missing' four years in the middle of the reign of Sethy II, it can be inferred that his reign in the south was interrupted by that of a usurper named Amenmesse – whose four years are included in the community records.

Another group of material from the archives of the Theban necropolis includes the records of the investigation under Rameses IX (Dynasty XX) of a series of major tomb robberies. These culminate in the minutes of the court proceedings against the culprits. Another set of judicial records cover the trial of individuals accused of the murder of Rameses III, a conspiracy that seems to have included attempts to use 'voodoo' dolls.

Most of these documents come from Thebes; the wetter conditions in the north of the country detracted from the preservation of papyrus and ink. Nevertheless, papyri have come to light from temple archives found at Abusir (Dynasty V) and also at the Dynasty XII site, Lahun/Kahun. A lot can be learned about temple administration from the accounts and priestly duty rosters found there. The rosters show that smaller sanctuaries lacked a full-time staff, and relied on local administrators, farmers and soldiers, who served as priests on a rota basis. Medical and veterinary treatises and the wills of members of the temple-community were also found.

Above: *The mortuary temple complex of Rameses III at Medinet Habu, which served as the headquarters of the administration of the huge necropolis, or cemetery area, at Thebes during Dynasties XX–XXI. It is an important source of documents, most of which were found in the early years of the nineteenth century. From here came the trial records of those accused of robbing some of the royal tombs.*

Below: *Village of Deir el-Medina. Dating from the New Kingdom, it was the home of the workmen and artists responsible for building the royal tombs in the Valley of the Kings. A vast range of documents has been recovered from the area. The village is in the foreground, while on the incline opposite were built the workers' own tombs, decorated with the same care and attention that they lavished on the pharaohs' sepulchres.*

Above: *Ostrakon from Thebes. Many administrative documents were written on papyrus, but slivers of limestone, known as ostraka, were also used, usually inscribed in hieratic script.*

EXPEDITION RECORDS

Above: The tombs of the governors of Aswan on the hill of Qubbet el-Hawa opposite their city. The governors were the greatest explorers of their day, and their tombs contain accounts of many of their journeys into the heart of Africa.

A lot of the state's energy and resources was devoted to expeditions into the desert regions of Egypt. When their expedition was completed, leaders would leave behind inscribed records of their activities at the site. A particularly frequent destination was the Wadi Hammamat, in the Eastern Desert, from which greywacke, a stone much used for statuary and sarcophagi, was quarried. In the reign of Montjuhotpe IV (end of Dynasty XI), the Vizier Amenemhat was sent there to procure stone for the royal sarcophagus; his inscription relates that:

> There came a gazelle great with young, going with her face before her, while her eyes looked backwards. She did not turn back, and arrived at this august moment, at this block, still in its place, that was intended to be the lid of the sarcophagus. She dropped her young upon it while the army of the king looked on. They sacrificed her upon the block, and made a fire.

With the encouragement of this omen, the block was safely quarried for its journey to Thebes.

Quarry texts are found around the many locations in which the Egyptians obtained stones, ores and other precious materials. Many such texts can be found in the Sinai Peninsula, where copper and turquoise were mined. The earliest texts there date to the beginning of Dynasty III, the latest to Dynasty XX, and follow the usual kinds of patterns of royal names, offering scenes and

Below: The Tomb of Harkhuf, one of Aswan's governors. Included on its facade is a copy of a letter he received from his young king.

Above: Inscription from the Wadi Maghara. Another kind of expedition record is provided by the graffiti left by various quarrying expeditions. Some of the earliest examples are in the Sinai, where turquoise was mined; this one shows Seneferu slaying an enemy.

other records of the quarry workers. However, from the Second Intermediate Period come some extremely strange texts. Known as 'Protosinaitic', they comprise signs that appear at first sight to be hieroglyphs, but do not, in fact, belong to the Egyptian corpus. Their limited number suggests a true alphabetic script, with the forms of the signs derived from certain Egyptian hieroglyphs, but with different meanings. It has been argued that they form the direct ancestors of the later Phoenician/Canaanite alphabet, but although some words have been read plausibly, confirmation is yet lacking.

Examples have also been found in Palestine, but recent work by John and Deborah Darnell has now brought to light examples of the script much further south, in the Wadi el-Hol, part of a desert caravan track north-west of Luxor. These also date to Middle Kingdom times, and raise further questions as to the origins and purpose of these mysterious inscriptions.

Above: *The necropolis at Thebes, intended destination of Montjuhotpe IV's sarcophagus. The Deir el-Bahari temples are towards the right, with private tomb chapels of the New Kingdom in the centre.*

Below: *Wadi Hammamat, a major quarrying area, whose stone was particularly popular for the manufacture of sarcophagi. This ram was carved by quarrymen working in Year 3 of Psametik II.*

WISDOM AND PHILOSOPHY

Above: *King Khufu, the builder of the Great Pyramid at Giza and second ruler of Dynasty IV. In his reign lived one of the earliest known authors of 'wisdom literature', Prince Djedefhor.*

A type of text related to autobiography is 'wisdom literature', in which the author gives advice to his descendants. These texts are found throughout Egyptian history, the earliest surviving example probably dating to Dynasty V, but attributed to the Dynasty IV Prince Hordjedef, son of Khufu, builder of the Great Pyramid. They advise 'proper' behaviour towards one's fellow citizens, and respect for all. Gluttony and arrogance are abhorred; modesty and charity are recommended; sexual temptation is warned against.

As time went by, these compositions become less idealistic and more utilitarian. One of the latest examples, the 'Instructions of Ankhshoshenqy' (Ptolemaic Period) replaces the elegant stanzas of the earliest works with one-line sayings, some of which are of a distinctly misogynistic flavour; contrast advice of the Dynasty XIX scribe, Any, to *'not control your wife in your house ... recognize her skill'*, with Ankhshoshenqy's claim that *'[i]nstructing a woman is like having a sack of sand whose side is split open'*.

A curious genre of 'philosophical' literature that was particularly popular in the Middle Kingdom is the so-called 'pessimistic literature', where an author laments the condition of the world. The meaning of such texts has been much debated, the main question being how far they are a literary device, and how much a reflection of events that had accompanied the civil wars of the preceding First Intermediate Period. Either way, the 'Lamentation of Ipuwer' paints a lurid picture of the country:

Lo, the face is pale, the bowmen ready,
Crime is everywhere, there is no man of yesterday ...
Lo, Hapy inundates and none plough for him,
All say, "We know not what has happened to the land" ...
Lo, poor men have become men of wealth,
He who could not buy sandals now owns riches ...
Lo, hearts are violent, a storm sweeps the land,
Blood is everywhere, there is no shortage of dead ...
Lo, many dead are buried in the river,
The stream is the grave, the grave is the stream,
Lo, nobles lament, the poor rejoice,
Every town says, "Let us expel our rulers"...
See now, men rebel against the Serpent,
Stolen is the crown of Re, who pacifies the Two Lands ...
See the royal residence is fearful from want ...
The troops we raised for ourselves have become Bowmen, bent on destroying!

A similar tone pervades a number of other types of text, for example the 'Harpers Songs', which cast a jaundiced eye upon life and death. One seems

Above: *A scribe of Dynasty V, one of the periods when 'wisdom literature' flourished.*

to even doubt the belief in eternal life that so characterizes the ancient Egyptians, and adopts the philosophy of 'eat, drink and be merry, for tomorrow we die':

> The nobles and spirits are entombed in their pyramids,
> They built chapels, but their shrines are no more: what has become of them?
> I have heard the sayings of [wise men], which are quoted to this day:
> Where are their shrines? Their walls have fallen and their shrines are gone.
> There is no one who can come back from [the next world] to tell us how they fare,
> To comfort us until we reach the place where they have gone.
> So ... follow your desires while you live;
> Place myrrh on your head, cloth yourself in fine linen ...
> Remember, one cannot take his goods with him;
> None goes away and then comes back.

Following pages: Detail of wall painting from the tombs of the workmen. A harper plays for the Foreman of the Royal Tomb workmen, Anhurkhau, and his wife, Waab, in their burial chamber at Deir el-Medina.

Below: Scenes of celebration on the 'Red Chapel' erected by Hatshepsut at Karnak.

HUMAN RELATIONSHIPS

In contrast to these gloomy thoughts, Egyptian love songs and poetry celebrate the here and now. Egyptian marriages were arranged between parents while the couple were still children, but love-matches were still idealized.

> 'He stares me out when I walk by, and all alone I cry for joy; how happy is my delight with the lover in my sight ...'; 'Hearing your voice is pomegranate wine, for I live to hear it; every glance (of yours) which rests on me means more to me than food and drink ...'.

There are many documents of this kind, some of which are riddled with double-entendres, particularly with references to ladies' 'grottos'. Rather more prosaic are documents relating to the details of relationships. There seems to have been no 'marriage ceremony' as such: the woman simply moved into

Below: *The Overseers of the Manicurists Niankhkhnum and Khnumhetep, from their joint tomb at Saqqara. The nature of their relationship is uncertain, but the image has an intimacy not usually seen on more regal monuments.*

Right: *Letters from the Dynasty XI mortuary-priest Heqanakhte. The papyri are written in hieratic, in columns. Soon afterwards, this practice ceased for day-to-day documents, in favour of horizontal lines.*

her husband's house. However, wills and adoptions can be traced through documents from towns such as Deir el-Medina and Kahun. One interesting set relates how a childless couple purchased a slave, with whom the husband fathered a number of children, who then became his heirs. There are also the usual small-town stories of domestic scandals that allow us to know more about the citizens of Deir el-Medina than those of any other settlement of early antiquity. Some individuals are so well known that their handwriting alone is enough to identify a document: the Dynasty XX scribe Djhutmose and his son Butehamun, for example, and the rather earlier Qenhirkopshef, who is easily identified by his atrocious script!

Even earlier is the correspondence sent by the Dynasty XI/XII mortuary priest, Heqanakhte, to his son, covering aspects of running the family farm and other domestic issues. The situation revealed about the relationships within the household inspired Agatha Christie to use it as the basis for her novel, *Death Comes as an End!*

Below: *The tomb of the Vizier Ipi at Deir el-Bahari, just left of the path. The private archive of his priest Heqanakhte was found in front of the tomb, where it had been discarded for some reason by Heqanakhte's son and deputy.*

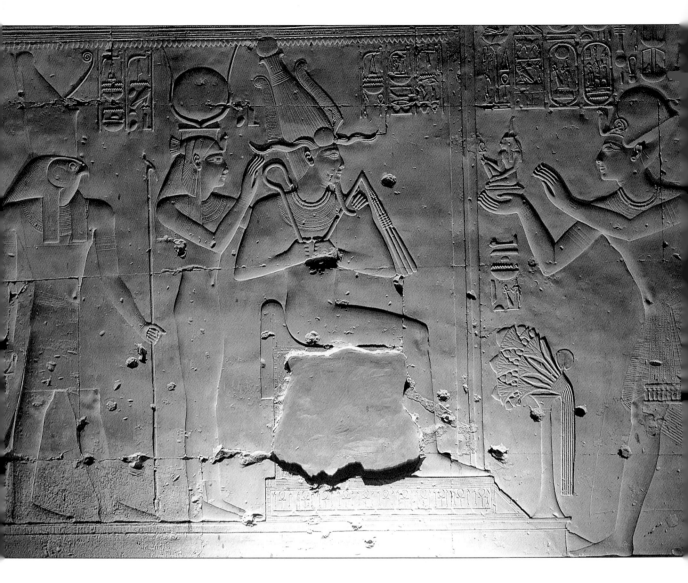

STORIES

Above: *The gods Horus, Isis and Osiris from the temple of Sethy I at Abydos. One of the best-known stories from ancient Egypt was the myth of the god of the dead, Osiris, which told of his murder by his brother, Seth, his rescue by his sister-wife, Isis, and the vengeance carried out by his son, Horus.*

Alongside all these written sources is a wide range of stories. Most were doubt-less told by public story-tellers long before being written down. We can often see this from the way that the tales are put together, with frequent repeti-tions, and a more-or-less poetic make-up. Some may be heavily-embroidered accounts of real events (such as the 'Story of Sinuhe', *see page 69*); others contain a kernel of political propaganda.

A good example of the latter is the Westcar Papyrus (named, like many other papyri, after its first modern owner), a Second Intermediate Period copy of what was originally an Old Kingdom story. It is given the form of a cycle of stories of magic told to amuse the bored King Khufu. They are related by his sons, and conclude with one which tells of the birth of triplets, fathered by the sun-god, Re, who will one day be kings. The triplets are actually the

THE STORY OF THE SHIPWRECKED SAILOR

A classic of Egyptian literature is the tale known as the 'Story of the Shipwrecked Sailor'. It opens with a sailor trying to comfort a colleague who has just returned from a disastrous expedition. The sailor tells how his ship was sunk in a storm, with the loss of all of its crew apart from himself. He is washed up on an island where he meets a giant snake. Although terrifying to look at, the snake is friendly, and the sole survivor of his family, the rest of whom had been killed by a falling meteorite. Sympathizing with the sailor for the loss of all his shipmates, he loads him with gifts, and correctly prophesies that a ship will pass and pick up the castaway. The sailor ends up being presented to the king and promoted. Unfortunately, his attempts to show his colleague that 'all's well that ends well' are of no avail: the latter dismisses him with the remark 'Don't try and be clever with me: who gives water to a goose just before it is killed?' He knows that he is to be punished for his failure (the nature of which is not revealed in the surviving copy of the story).

Right: Model boat from the tomb of the Chancellor Meketre at Thebes. This is one of the finest examples of an artefact that was common placed in Middle Kingdom tombs.

first rulers of Dynasty V, and the story was clearly composed under the last of them to show that his family was of divine origin.

On the other hand, some stories are simply for entertainment. More than one contains elements found in stories across several continents: princesses locked up in towers, princes in disguise and quests for magical items. Allegories such as 'The Blinding of Truth by Falsehood' and others demonstrate the victory of good over evil. Stories featuring gods are common: more than one tells of the conflict between Horus and his uncle Seth, the murderer of Osiris. Some of these formed the basis for theatrical performances during festivals, such as that related in the autobiography of Ikhernofret (*see page 68–9*) .

TEXTS OF MAGIC AND MEDICINE

Opposite: The temple of Sobk and Harouris at Kom Ombo. This relief shows various medical instruments, from the Ptolemaic Period.

Below: Greco-Roman Period mummy. The Egyptians were well known in the ancient world as physicians. The medical papyri include many examples of treatment for trauma. The owner of this mummy had lost an arm early in life, an injury which had clearly been successfully treated. The embalmers had provided him with a prosthetic arm for use in the afterlife.

In the ancient world, the Egyptians were renowned as physicians, and records exist of Egyptian doctors being sent abroad to treat highly-placed foreigners. Amongst the myriad papyri that have survived are a number which deal with the treatment of disease. These provide a fascinating mixture of what we would regard as proper 'medical' procedures, and those which we would dismiss as 'magic'. However, one must be wary of making such pejorative divisions based on modern scientific knowledge. In an era where the mechanism of disease transmission was unknown, and existence of supernatural beings was regarded as fact, 'magical' practices were perfectly logical. Indeed, given the importance of a patient's attitude to successful treatment, the rituals sometimes carried out may indeed have had a positive result.

The 'real' medicine in the papyri deals with injuries and conditions that clearly had an external cause or manifestation. One of the most important of such documents is the Edwin Smith Surgical Papyrus, now in New York, a systematic guide to the examination and treatment of various conditions. It describes the examination procedures, states whether or not treatment is possible, and then gives instructions as to how to carry out any treatment.

Other papyri have a rather less systematic approach, and are often general compilations of remedies for a range of conditions, although there are a number that concentrate on particular themes, for example gynaecology, or snake bites.

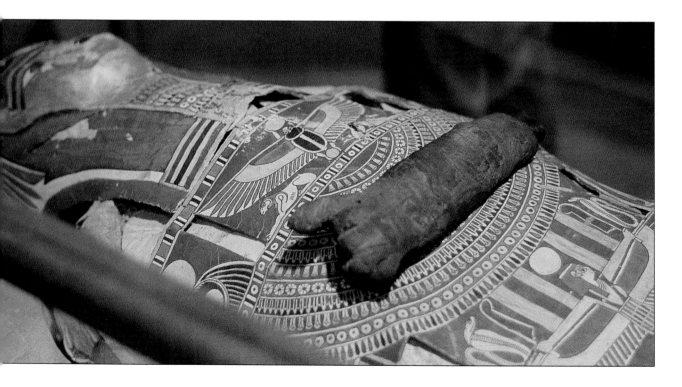

Above: *The tomb of the Steward Kheruef from Dynasty XVIII. The ancient Egyptians were themselves amongst the earliest tourists, and left their graffiti on the ancient monuments they visited. Here an ink-written hieratic graffito has been added to the carved façade of the tomb.*

THE END OF THE ANCIENT LANGUAGE

The various scripts of the Egyptian language remained unchallenged in Egypt until the end of the Late Period, when the country fell under the yoke of foreign empires. Following Alexander the Great's conquest in 332 BC, and the establishment of the Macedonian Greek dynasty of the Ptolemies, there was a steady influx of Greek settlers. With the ruling class composed of Greeks, Greek writing became widely used. It served with demotic as the main administrative medium, and appeared alongside it and hieroglyphic text on a number of monumental decrees, such as the Rosetta Stone and Decree of Canopus.

However, hieroglyphs and hieratic were by now largely restricted to religious uses, and it is clear that knowledge of them became more and more restricted as time went by. Temples continued to be built with the ancient religious images and texts, but they were using a version of the language that was now some 1500 years old, and bore little or no relation to the current speech. All that kept the ancient script alive was the religion whose dogma it was used to enshrine.

Pressure on the ancient script was further increased by the inexorable spread of the Christian religion through the country. The last great stronghold of paganism was the temple-isle of Philae, the cult-centre of the goddess Isis since the Late Period, and it was there, in AD 394, that the last dated hieroglyphic inscription was carved, 82 years after the Empire became Christian. Paganism maintained a tenuous toe-hold at Philae, and at Siwa in the Western Desert until AD 553, when the final sanctuaries were forcibly closed. However,

Above: *Part of the temple of Maharraqa in Nubia. Although temples continued to be built in the ancient style during the Roman Period, knowledge of the ancient scripts gradually declined.*

Left: *The Temple at Philae: the final stronghold of paganism in Egypt.*

Above right: *The Gate of Hadrian at Philae. The last known hieroglyphic inscription of antiquity, was carved here in* AD *394.*

Above and below: *With the decipherment of ancient Egyptian, more faithful pastiches were produced, one of the best being the inscription placed next to the entrance of the Great Pyramid at Giza by Lepsius.*

by then the last demotic text had also been written, again at Philae, in AD 452. Writing in Egypt was by then either in Greek or Coptic, and within 200 years, increasingly in Arabic as well. Hieroglyphic script now slumbered.

HIEROGLYPHS FOR THE MODERN AGE

It was not until 1,400 years after the last ancient hieroglyphic inscription had been written that knowledge of the script was regained (*see Chapter V*). This knowledge has largely been diverted towards the study of texts written in ancient times, but there have been examples of new texts being composed.

Possibly the earliest of these is to be found at the Great Pyramid at Giza, where a large, well-cut hieroglyphic inscription is to be found to the top right of the entrance to the monument. Rather than King Khufu, the founder of the pyramid, it commemorates the king of Prussia, Friedrich Wilhelm IV (1840–61), and was inscribed by the Prussian Egyptologist Carl Richard Lepsius (*see page 119–20*), who led a great scientific expedition to Egypt from 1842–5.

Since then, such new texts have appeared elsewhere in the world. Most spectacularly, in the 1980s, the zoo in Memphis, Tennessee, USA, built its new gate in the form of a temple pylon in celebration of its namesake, the ancient capital of Egypt. For this, scholars at the University of Memphis translated the zoo's Mission Statement into Middle Egyptian, which was then carved in hieroglyphs onto the façades and architraves of the gateway, a magnificent reminder of the enduring power of ancient Egypt and its age-old script.

Below: The front façade to Memphis Zoo, Memphis, Tennessee. The zoo's mission statement, translated into Middle Egyptian, is colourfully displayed on the gateway. This is perhaps the most impressive example of the modern use of hieroglyphs.

Above centre: Modern cartouche at Giza. Made for King Farouq, the penultimate ruler of modern Egypt, this new cartouche is affixed to the gates of the former royal rest-house, now a cafeteria, just in front of the Great Pyramid.

Right: The Penzance Egyptian House, built for John Lavin in 1835, just as interest in ancient Egypt was re-ignited. While the overall arrangement is derived from Egyptian concepts, the female 'deity' busts look rather more akin to ships' figureheads.

CHAPTER IV

THE MYSTERY OF THE HIEROGLYPHS

Hieroglyphs Eclipsed

Above: *Temple of Isis at Philae. With the victory of Christianity, many pagan temples were converted to churches. Here, the cross has been carved on top of the sacred texts of the cult of Isis.*

ENERAL KNOWLEDGE of the hieroglyphic script contracted rapidly during Roman times. Its use was effectively limited to the walls of temples, and so to the restricted world of the priesthood. In these circumstance, the existing belief held by Greek and Roman writers that hieroglyphs were somehow something more mysterious than simple letters gained further support.

Earlier Classical writers broadly supported the view that hieroglyphs were a true system of writing, and even that they were the ancestors of all alphabets. Plato and others attributed its invention to a 'a certain Theuth' (the ibis-god Thoth). However, they clearly had difficulty in seeing the hieroglyphs as a phonetic script, or in distinguishing actual hieroglyphs from parts of the scenes that they frequently accompany. This was because very few Greeks and Romans, even if living in Egypt, learned the script. Most would simply use Greek, the language of government; a few might venture into demotic, but hieroglyphs lay outside their sphere. Thus, Classical scholars conceived hieroglyphs as symbolic, not

> *'express[ing] the intended concept by means of syllables joined one to another, but by means of the significance of the objects which have been copied, and by its figurative meaning that has been impressed on the memory by practice'.*

This view was expressed by the Roman historian Diodorus Siculus, writing in the middle of the first century BC, at a time when temples were still being constructed covered with texts in hieroglyphs. Over subsequent centuries, there was no change in this generally held view.

FROM ALEXANDER TO NAPOLEON

PTOLEMAIC PERIOD

332–30 BC
Egypt ruled by heirs of Alexander the Great

ALEXANDER THE GREAT IN EGYPTIAN GUISE, KARNAK

ROMAN PERIOD

30 BC–AD 395
Egypt made a Roman Province

HELLENISTIC SPHINX OF THE 2ND CENTURY AD

COPTIC PERIOD

AD 395–640
Egypt part of the Eastern Empire, based on Constantinople

Above: *Temple at Wadi el-Sebua in Nubia. One of the temples later converted into a church, it had been originally built by Rameses II, who had been shown offering flowers either side of the niche at the back, which had held the divine images.*

Right: *Detail from Temple at Wadi el-Sebua. When the temple was converted, everything was coated in whitewash, and a figure of St Peter, holding a massive key, painted in the niche. The whitewash has now partly fallen away, leaving the appearance that it is the saint who is the recipient of Rameses' gifts!*

ARAB PERIOD

AD 640–1517
The General Amr conquers Egypt for the Kaliphs

INSCRIPTION OF THE KALIPH EL-MUSTANSIR,
DATED 1084–5 AD

OTTOMAN PERIOD

AD 1517–1805
The Turkish Sultan Selim I invades and incorporates the country into his Empire

TOMBS OF THE OTTOMAN PERIOD
IN CAIRO

Above: *The Christian cathedral at Qasr Ibrim in Nubia. It is the last part of Lower Nubia to remain above the surface of Lake Nasser, and originally towered over the river.*

Above: *Statue of Thoth in his chapel in the catacomb of his sacred animals at Tunah el-Gebel. A lunar god, Thoth was sometimes shown as a baboon with the crescent moon on his head. He was later equated with Hermes.*

There were some honourable exceptions to this state of ignorance. One was Chairemon (*fl.*mid-first century AD) who had lived in Alexandria, and described various signs with meanings that are not too far from the truth, although tied up in a symbolic world view. Clement of Alexandria (*c.*AD 150 – AD 215) seems to have recognized the existence of phonetic signs, although only in an overall symbolic and allegorical context and a translation of the text on an obelisk at Rome (now in the Piazza del Popolo) by a certain Hermapion in the middle of the third century, later quoted by the Roman historian Ammanius Marcellinus (*c.*AD 330–60), is broadly correct. However, by this time, the philosopher Plotinus (AD 205–70) had set out the theory which was to underpin European hieroglyphic studies for one and a half millennia. Plotinus suggested that rather than representing ordinary letters expressing sounds that went on to make up words, hieroglyphs were images from which the initiated could gain a fundamental insight into the very essence of things.

These conceptions became bound up in various allegedly 'Egyptian' philosophical speculations, known as the 'Hermetic Corpus' after the Greek god Hermes who was equated with Thoth. Although purely Greek in origin, these ideas formed the foundation of later work, and were in many ways instrumental in delaying the decipherment of hieroglyphs.

Another hindrance was the survival of a work by Horapollo, an Egyptian, probably written around the fourth century and known as the *Hieroglyphica*. It has 179 chapters, each dealing with a single hieroglyph or concept, and often contains a frustrating mixture of half-truth and non-Egyptian metaphysical speculation. For example, according to Horapollo, the vulture and

the goose are said to mean 'mother' and 'son', respectively. This is quite true, but for purely phonetic reasons, not because 'male vultures do not exist' or 'geese love their offspring more than any other'! There are a fair number of similar examples where a sign's usage is correctly identified, albeit for unlikely reasons, but there are also examples of imaginary signs or completely wrong-headed interpretations. It is clear that Horapollo had access to something akin to contact with those who still understood hieroglyphs, but lacked that understanding himself. His work was a classic example of the kind of account produced by someone with a passing acquaintance with a subject, but without the insight to understand his limitations. Horapollo's work was lost from the end of antiquity down to its rediscovery in the fifteenth century, but was subsequently printed and regarded by almost all scholars as the only 'authentic' account of the hieroglyphs.

THE RENAISSANCE VIEW

During the Middle Ages, interest in hieroglyphs slumbered. In Egypt, the absolute victory of Christianity, and its widespread replacement by Islam after AD 640, meant that the old scripts were utterly obsolete and all knowledge lost. In the west, ancient Egypt and its works were seen only through the fog of the biblical narrative and odd fragments of classical writings. Thus, in the mosaics of St Mark's Cathedral, Venice, built in the late eleventh century, the pyramids are the granaries of Joseph.

However, with the Renaissance, a real interest in the past became manifest, including a desire to reconcile Christian and ancient philosophies. A number of classical texts were rediscovered, including views on Egypt and its hieroglyphs; of particular importance was Plutarch's work on the myth of the god of the dead, Osiris, and his wife, Isis. The work of Horapollo (*see above*) was found on the Greek island of Andros in 1419. Horapollo's view of hieroglyphs thus became central to the learned view of them during the Renaissance and beyond; indeed, 15 editions of Horapollo were to appear during the sixteenth century.

The Horapolloan conception of hieroglyphs became mixed in with the creation of new 'hieroglyphs'. These were intended to provide architectural ornamentation that expressed ideas which be read and understood by initiated scholars. Although they neither copied or were even based upon genuine

Above left: The sarcophagus made for the last native Egyptian pharaoh, Nakhthorheb. Pharaonic monuments became objects of curiosity, to be re-used where appropriate. This sarcophagus was used as part of an ablution fountain in the Attarin Mosque in Alexandria.

Above right: The Rafai Mosque in Cairo. The decisive break with the past came with the Arab invasion of Egypt in AD 640. With the victory of Islam, Arabic gradually replaced Coptic as the general language of the country.

Above: Francesco Colonna's Egyptian fantasy. His invented hieroglyphs were of considerable influence during the sixteenth century, although, as may be clearly seen, they bore no resemblance to the real thing.

POINTING THE WAY

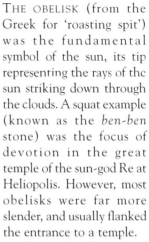

THE OBELISK (from the Greek for 'roasting spit') was the fundamental symbol of the sun, its tip representing the rays of the sun striking down through the clouds. A squat example (known as the *ben-ben* stone) was the focus of devotion in the great temple of the sun-god Re at Heliopolis. However, most obelisks were far more slender, and usually flanked the entrance to a temple.

The earliest known example was erected by Teti (Dynasty VI) at Heliopolis, although the oldest one still standing is that of Senwosret I (Dynasty XII), also at Heliopolis. Most obelisks were quarried from the granite of Aswan, and carried on barges downstream to the temples of Thebes, Memphis, Heliopolis, Pirameses, and other cities further north. The transport of one pair of Karnak obelisks is depicted in the Dynasty XVIII temple of Hatshepsut at Deir el-Bahari. It is generally agreed that the actual erection took place by dragging the obelisk to the top of a ramp, below which was a sand-box. Sand was allowed to escape from the latter, gently lowering the obelisk into place. A televised experiment carried out in the USA has now proved the efficacy of the technique.

Obelisks were generally decorated with the names and titles of the king who ordered them to be erected, together with some statement on his or her dedication of the monument to the gods. The last examples were produced in the Roman Period, during which time many earlier obelisks were transported to Rome for re-erection. There, they played an important role in the early attempts at deciphering the hieroglyphs.

Above: *Rameses II's entrance to the temple of Luxor. The obelisk's associations are reinforced by figures of baboons on the base adoring the rising sun.*

Top right: *Temple at Karnak. The surviving obelisks of Thutmose I and Hatshepsut tower over the central area of the temple.*

Left: *The obelisks of Hatshepsut are amongst the best documented in existence. Their quarrying is recorded in the female king's temple at Deir el-Bahari, while their dedication is commemorated on this quartzite block from her 'Red Chapel' at Karnak.*

Egyptian hieroglyphs, these new signs became intimately mingled with speculations related to the real ancient script. An example of the confusion over what constituted real hieroglyphs is shown by the frequent reproduction of an 'Egyptian text' on a Roman temple frieze from Rome, and a widespread belief that the invented hieroglyphs in an illustrated fantasy by Francesco Colonna (1433–1527) were copies of actual inscriptions!

During the sixteenth century, an increasing number of scholars began to take an interest in hieroglyphs. An important stage was reached with the publication in 1556 of the *Hierogliphica* by Pierius Valerianus (1477–*c*.1560), a compilation of a series of 58 of his works on the subject, previously produced separately. Each deals with a specific hieroglyph, or group of hieroglyphs, and uses the now-traditional method of allegory to explain them. Explanations were thus far from the mark, yet the erudition displayed in the work, referencing some 200 authors, marks its importance. It was subsequently reprinted in more than one language, and remained a key reference source for a century.

The century also brought to light more genuine Egyptian texts, through the re-erection of a considerable number of obelisks at Rome. These had been brought there by the Roman emperors, overthrown at the end of antiquity, and then rediscovered and re-erected by a succession of Renaissance popes. The process continued into the seventeenth century; one of the men most closely associated with the works, Athanasius Kircher, being perhaps the key figure in the speculations concerning hieroglyphs in this period.

KIRCHER'S FLIGHT OF FANCY
Athanasius Kircher (1601–80) was a polymath, whose interests covered a whole range of scientific and humanist subjects. His interest in Egyptian antiq-

uities was kindled by seeing a book containing pictures of the obelisks in Rome, which inspired him to attempt to decipher their inscriptions. However, his first work on the Egyptian language was focused on Coptic, manuscripts and knowledge of which had begun to come to the west early in the seventeenth century. Kircher had been entrusted with the publication of manuscripts brought back by Pietro della Valle (1582–1652), an Italian nobleman and traveller, and produced an introduction to the Coptic tongue in 1636. Although a number of Kircher's conclusions were incorrect,

Above: Relief from the temple of Sethy I at Abydos. The ibis-headed Thoth, god of writing and wisdom, revivifies the resurrected Osiris.

Below: The Roman 'birth house' temple at Dendara. Emperor Augustus, depicted as a pharaoh, makes offerings to Isis and her son, Horus. Egyptian cults, especially that of Isis, spread to Rome itself.

Above: Medal made for Sixtus V (1585–90). The obverse shows the monuments placed at the Vatican, Lateran, Piazza Popolo and on the Esquiline in Rome. Interest in the hieroglyphs was re-engendered in the sixteenth and seventeenth centuries, when various popes re-erected a number of the obelisks that had been brought to Rome in Imperial times. Pope Sixtus V was the greatest of the obelisk-pontiffs.

Above centre: Obelisk outside the Church of San Giovanni, Lateran, Rome. It is the largest of all the surviving Egyptian obelisks.

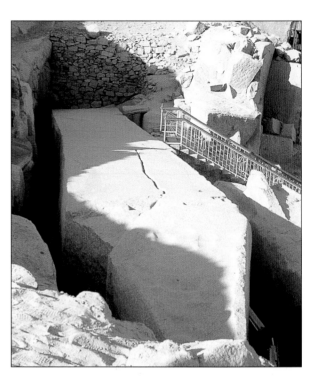

Above: The intended mate of the Lateran obelisk. It still lies in its quarry at Aswan. A flaw in the rock led to its rejection and abandonment by the ancient craftsmen.

the book contained the fundamental observation that Coptic and ancient Egyptian were the same language. A further volume, published in 1644, provided a far more in-depth account of Coptic, and became the basis for all study of the language in the immediately succeeding decades.

In 1650, Kircher was further entrusted with the publication of a study of the obelisk then being re-erected in the Piazza Navona (*see page 103*), one of the latest known, and (as we now know) carved for the Emperor Domitian (AD 81–96). Kircher also studied other obelisks and Egyptian material in Rome. He began from a belief in the close equivalence between classical and Egyptian mythologies, and that a correct idea of Egyptian philosophical conceptions had been preserved in the works of the classical and other writers. On the basis that the classical sources had also said that the hieroglyphic script contained the esoteric knowledge of the Egyptians, Kircher thus felt that he knew in advance what hieroglyphic texts said, and it was simply a question of determining how the one could be derived from the other.

In doing so, Kircher regarded the hieroglyphs as symbols, yet also believed that there was a parallel 'vulgar' usage, that might be basically alphabetical. While his limited work in this direction was based on wholly-wrong assumptions, there was one flash of insight which allowed him to read the group ⌇⌇ as 'm' (actually 'mw' – 'water') – the first time that a hieroglyph had been read for over a thousand years.

Unluckily, the vast majority of Kircher's efforts was directed towards the non-existent 'symbolic' use of hieroglyphs, that based their meaning on allegory, understandable only by initiates. Each hieroglyph was assigned a philosophical concept or demonological manifestation, and then examined within the cosmos that Kircher had constructed out of the material available to him. Thus in his publication of the Navona obelisk, the Emperor's alphabetically-written cartouche was 'translated' as follows: '*The beneficent generative force commanding through supernal and infernal dominion, augments the flow of sacred humour emanating from above. Saturn, the disposer of fleeting time, promotes the fecundity of the soil, commanding humid nature. For by his influence all things have life and force*'.

While to modern eyes absurd, Kircher's conclusions were based on a scholarly method, the pity being that the method was so badly chosen; but Kircher was by no means the last scholar to be led astray.

THE FIRST GLIMMERS OF ENLIGHTENMENT

The philosophic ideas that underpinned Kircher's work were already under attack during his lifetime, principally through demonstrations that the Hermetic works were in no way derived from ancient Egypt. Following on from this came scepticism over whether the hieroglyphs were indeed the esoteric repositories of priestly learning.

Above: *The site of the Lateran Obelisk. Having lain by the Sacred Lake in Karnak temple for nearly 30 years, the Lateran obelisk was finally erected here by Thutmose IV, at the easternmost end of the temple. It stood alone, as a symbol of the sun.*

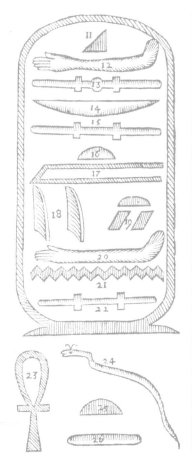

Left: *The title page of Athanasius Kircher's* Obeliscus Pamphilius *(Rome, 1650),* which published his conclusions on an obelisk re-erected in the Piazza Navona.

Right: *Obelisk in the Piazza Navona, Rome. This monument was one of the latest of its type, having been carved and erected for the Roman Emperor Domitian.*

Above: *Kircher's (inaccurate) copy of Domitian's cartouche on the Navona obelisk. This he interpreted as reading:* 'The beneficent generative force commanding through supernal and infernal dominion, augments the flow of sacred humour emanating from above. Saturn, the disposer of fleeting time, promotes the fecundity of the soil, commanding humid nature. For by his influence all things have life and force'. *The cartouche and the signs that follow it actually read:* 'Kasaros Temiytyanos [Caesar Domitianus], who lives for ever'.

Early in the eighteenth century came recognition of the existence of cursive Egyptian scripts, while a conceptual step forward is to be seen in Book IV of *The Divine Legation of Moses* (1740), by William Warburton, later Bishop of Gloucester (1698–1779). In this, he set out the view that scripts developed from pure pictograms to 'contrasted and arbitrarily instituted marks' in a steady manner. The Abbé Jean Jacques Barthélemy (1716–95) took this concept, and demonstrated that some hieroglyphs could indeed be the ancestors of hieratic signs. In a paper published in 1761, the Abbé also observed that cartouches might contain royal and divine names. Warburton also proposed the existence of a number of types of hieroglyph, including ideograms and determinatives, as well as making the case for the script having been designed not for 'sacred secrets', but for day-to-day purposes. Nevertheless, he did not make any attempt to apply his concepts to actual texts.

Alongside these rejections of the stale theories of the Renaissance came other fruitless avenues of speculation. The eighteenth century displayed a further expansion of the literature concerning Egyptian writing, one theme, pursued by the English academic John Needham (1713–81), being the equation of Egyptian and Chinese, based on a so-called 'bust of Isis' that actually bore neither Egyptian nor Chinese characters! A considerable number of others followed a similar route. Joseph de Guignes (1721–1800) made China an Egyptian colony, and their languages originally identical. He dismissed

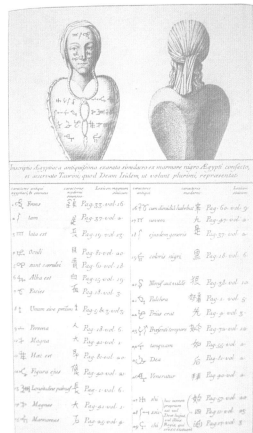

Coptic as so corrupted by its links with Greek as to be useless from the point of view of decipherment. De Guignes' views remained popular throughout the century, one major proponent being the Swedish diplomat Count Nils Gustaf Palin (1765–1842), who wrote several volumes on the subject between 1802 and 1812.

More helpful was the growing corpus of copies of real Egyptian texts, in particular those brought back by travellers to the Near East. Carsten Niebuhr (1733–1815) spent 1761–2 in Egypt and made accurate copies that enabled him to produce a table showing a selection of hieroglyphs, sorted by kind.

Barthélemy's observations on the import of cartouches were reinforced over 35 years later, by the work of the Danish antiquarian Jørgen Zoëga (1755–1809). In 1797, he published a study of the Roman obelisks for Pope Pius VI, a massive tome that included an in-depth discussion of the hiero-glyphs. Zoëga recognized the significance of the direction in which a hieroglyph faced to indicate which way a text ran and, most critically, that some signs might be purely phonetic. However, he went too far in suggesting that the final pre-Coptic variant of the script (demotic) might have become alphabetic. In spite of his insights, Zoëga did not actually try to decipher the script; rather, he drew a line under what had come before and provided an intellectual springboard towards true decipherment. Within a year of the publi-cation of his book, the key to the mystery of the hieroglyphs had been found.

Above: The notorious 'Bust of Isis', in Turin. It had been classified as 'Egyptian' on the grounds that the characters it bore were hieroglyphs; a number of writers, including John Needham, then interpreted them as Chinese, thus proposing identity between the two scripts. In fact, the signs signify the zodiac, there being nothing to even link the image with Egypt!

CHAPTER V

DECIPHERMENT OF THE HIEROGLYPHS

The Key is Found

Above: *Napoleon Bonaparte inspecting a mummy during his 1798 Egyptian expedition. Napoleon's military ambitions produced an unexpected result for Egyptology.*

Opposite: *Queen Hatshepsut's obelisk at Karnak. This is part of the dedication inscription, showing the hieroglyphic style of the XVIII Dynasty.*

IN SPITE OF THE MODEST PROGRESS in the study of hieroglyphs during the last part of the eighteenth century, there remained a fundamental problem. There was no way of testing any of the theories or suggestions in a meaningful way. In short, unless one had an inscription or document in which the same material was provided in both hieroglyphs and in a known language written in a known script, there was little more that could be done to expand the field of knowledge.

Just such a pivotal document was ultimately provided during the French occupation of Egypt, begun by General Napoleon Bonaparte (later Emperor Napoleon I) on behalf of the French Republic in 1798. The expedition was primarily aimed against the United Kingdom; it was intended to provide a strategic base for an assault on British possessions in India. However, it also had the alleged 'higher' aim of 'improving the lot of the natives of Egypt', and exploring, mapping and recording the country. In addition to military and naval forces, teams of scientists, scholars and artists were also assembled to follow the advancing armies and capture Egypt for the world of knowledge. Their work was ultimately to be published in the vast, 19-volume *Description de l'Egypte*, which appeared between 1809 and 1822. This immense work provided for the first time a comprehensive, reliable documentation of the land of the Nile, and played an absolutely central role in the development of European interest in ancient Egypt. Together with the political changes that it also ushered into Egypt, the Napoleonic expedition is generally felt to be the first great turning point in the history of Egyptology.

COUNTDOWN TO UNDERSTANDING

AD 394
Last hieroglyphic text

LAST HIEROGLYPHS, PHILAE

AD 452
Last demotic text

1419
Rediscovery of Horapollo's work, lost since the fifth century

1636
Kircher publishes his first work

1740
Warburton writes on hieroglyphs

FRONTISPIECE OF KIRCHER'S FIRST WORK

1761
Barthélemy identifies link between hieratic and hieroglyphs

1798
Discovery of the Rosetta Stone

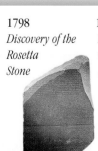

ROSETTA STONE

1814
Young identifies words within Rosetta Stone

1816
Bankes Obelisk found

1819
Young publishes first findings

BANKES OBELISK

1822
Champollion publishes first conclusions

JEAN-FRANCOIS CHAMPOLLION

1836–44
Champollion's dictionary and grammar conclusions published

1836
Lepsius publishes conclusions

Above: *The* Description de l'Égypte *was the enduring result of the militarily abortive Egyptian expedition. Bonaparte had brought a large team of scholars with his army, which undertook the first systematic survey of the country and its monuments. The results were published in nine volumes of text, and ten of plates between 1809 and 1822, and formed the springboard from which the subject of Egyptology then developed.*

The French expedition sailed from Toulon on 18 March 1878, captured Malta in June, and arrived near Alexandria at the end of the same month. Egypt's second city was rapidly captured, and within a short time the whole country was under French rule. However, the French were already trapped in Egypt as, on 1 August, a British fleet under Rear-Admiral Horatio Nelson had attacked the French fleet in Abuqir Bay, and destroyed it all except for two frigates.

Only a few days earlier, on 25 July, a slab of granite had been found during work on the construction of Fort Julien, just outside the north Delta town of Rashid. This was the location of one of the mouths of the Nile, and had been known to the Greeks as Rosetta. The slab bore three sets of text, in hieroglyphs, demotic script and Greek respectively. Luckily, its importance was instantly recognized by a French officer of the Engineers, Pierre-François-Xavier Bouchard (1772–1832), and it was sent to the Institute National in Cairo, set up by Bonaparte as part of his plan to transform Egypt into a modern country as the centre for scholarly work. At the Institute, the stone was inspected by the General himself, and copies made for dispatch to the leading scholars of Europe.

The stone was scheduled to be taken to France with the rest of the French expedition's antiquities, and was in the house of General Menou at Alexandria, when the French capitulated to the British forces led by Sir Ralph Abercromby in spring 1801. Ever since Nelson's destruction of the French fleet in 1798, the French position had been increasingly untenable, particularly following the landing of British troops in the country. Under Article XVI of the Treaty of Capitulation, all antiquities were to be ceded to the British, but Menou claimed that the stone was his own property in an attempt to prevent its removal. However, in October, a team of artillerymen were ultimately sent to take possession, and the stone was embarked in HMS *L'Égyptienne* (also an ex-French prize), and arrived at Portsmouth in February 1802. Moved to the Society of Antiquaries in London on 11 March, it then underwent intensive study. Within a month, a translation of the French text had been read to the Society, and in July casts were sent to Oxford, Cambridge, Edinburgh and Dublin Universities, with complete facsimiles being distributed around Europe. Towards the end of the year, the stone was moved once more, to its permanent home in British Museum.

YOUNG AND CHAMPOLLION

Real progress only came from the work of two individuals, the British physicist Thomas Young (1773–1829), and Jean-François Champollion (1790–1832) in France. Young was a polymath of the kind that no longer seems to exist today, a child prodigy who allegedly could read at the age of two, and

by 14 had a knowledge of a dozen languages. Initially trained as a doctor, he became an optical specialist who was elected a Fellow of the Royal Society at the age of 20. Two years later, he went to Göttingen to study physics, returning to England after being awarded his doctorate to study at Cambridge University. In 1799 he set up a medical practice in London .

Above: The town of Rashid (Rosetta), near the mouth of western branch of the Nile Delta. The all-important stone was discovered here.

Although a distinguished physician, Young's interests in physics and linguistics continued to develop. On the linguistic front, he was drawn to the problem of the Rosetta Stone, and in 1814 managed to divide large portions of the two Egyptian texts into specific words, with their Greek equivalents, and in November produced a conjectural translation of them. By the following year, he had prepared a demotic alphabet and a list of 86 demotic words, with their Greek equivalents. Importantly, he also recognized that the demotic, hieratic and hieroglyphic scripts were merely variants of the same writing system. This was based on his study of various manuscripts of the Book of the Dead, the religious text that accompanied many Egyptians to the grave from the New Kingdom onwards. The Book of the Dead has a very standardized formulation, and is found written in all three scripts; indeed, some are display signs that are half-way between hieroglyphic and hieratic. Careful study made it possible to see which hieroglyphic, hieratic and demotic signs were equivalent to one another, and to see differences between the ways that equivalent signs were used within different scripts.

Below: Napoleonic fortifications at Rosetta. It was here, in Fort Julien, that an inscribed slab was found in 1799.

In 1819, Young published a digest of his researches to date in a supplement to *Encyclopedia Britannica*. He had concluded that the hieroglyphic script used for writing foreign royal names was largely phonetic, rather than pictorial; he had determined the value of certain individual signs; and he had identified the cartouches of Ptolemy, Berinike and 'Tuthmosis' (= Thutmose). The latter was essentially a guess based on the appearance of an ibis within his cartouche: from Greek sources, it was known that this bird was sacred to the god Thoth. Unfortunately, having got so far, Young was unable to convince himself

THE ROSETTA STONE

THE ROSETTA STONE, as it is known, was once part of a stela, originally about 250 cm (98.4 inches) high and 80 cm (31.5 inches) wide, of which the top 30 cm (11.8 inches) or so is now missing, taking with it a considerable proportion of the Hieroglyphic text. The Demotic and Greek portions are, however, largely complete, and the latter was read immediately after the discovery as being a decree recounting the temple benefactions of King Ptolemy V, and dated to his ninth regnal year (196 BC). The key part from the point of view of the decipherment of ancient Egyptian scripts, however, was that the decree should be reproduced on a series of stelae, all

bearing the hieroglyphic, demotic and greek scripts, the first two writing the ancient Egyptian language, the last the Greek. Comparison of the three texts should thus, in theory at least, make the decipherment of the Egyptian texts fairly straightforward. Unfortunately, this was not to be the case.

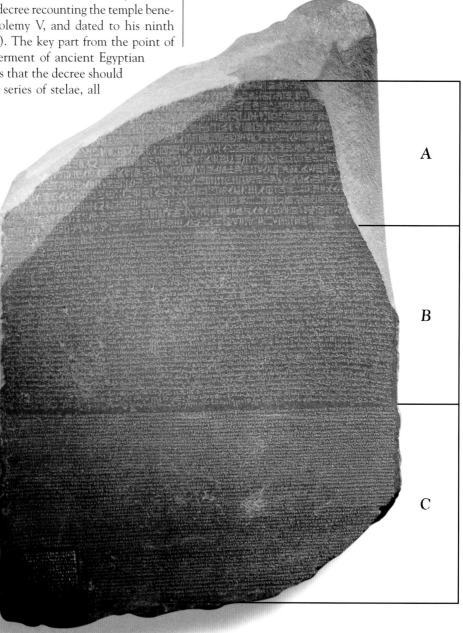

At first, scholars studying the Rosetta Stone concentrated on the demotic text in view of the amount of the hieroglyphic section that was missing. The fact that the script had been developed as simplified hand-written letters hid from most observers the direct relationship between it and the hieroglyphs. The general feeling was still that while the latter were an esoteric, 'symbolic' confection, demotic was likely to be 'real' writing. Nevertheless, Jean-Joseph Marcel (1776–1854) and Remi Raige, both members of the scientific commission that had accompanied the French army to Egypt, had recognized demotic as cursive hieroglyphs while the stone was still in Egypt.

The incompleteness of the hieroglyphic text may also have contributed to the delay in decoding the text. The first breakthrough came in 1802, with the work of the French orientalist Baron Antoine-Silvestre de Sacy (1758–1838) on the demotic text. He managed to isolate some of the proper names, but failed to explain them correctly. De Sacy's work was continued by the Swedish diplomat Johan David Åkerblad (1763–1819), who managed to establish the demotic groups for all proper names on the stone, as well for 'temples', 'Greeks' and 'him/his'. Unfortunately, Åkerblad was unable to go further, as he had assumed demotic to be a wholly alphabetic script. He had made important insights, however, unlike a number of other putative decipherers.

At one extreme, Tandeau de St Nicholas claimed that hieroglyphs were no more than decorative patterns, and not writing at all. Count Palin (*see page 103*) continued to advance his 'Chinese' theories, compounded with allegory. One of his suggestions was that the Psalms of David were Hebrew translations of Egyptian texts; this could be proved by translating the Hebrew text into Chinese(!), thus providing a key to the decipherment. Joseph von Hammer Purgstall (1774–1856) based his ideas on an Arabic treatise on certain enigmatic alphabets although they did not actually include hieroglyphs; on the other hand, he was one of the first adherents of the true decipherment when it came. Alexandre Lenoir (1762–1839) applied astronomical approaches to the hieroglyphs with less than happy results. Pierre Lacour (1779–1858) suggested that hieroglyphs were versions of Hebrew letters, and in turn the ancestors of the Greek alphabet.

These are but a few examples of the various strands of argument that ran in parallel with rather more productive researches.

A

Above: *The hieroglyphic section of the Rosetta Stone is the most severely damaged part, having lost more than half of its 29 lines, together with the images that would have been placed above the text.*

B

Above: *The demotic section of the Stone was that first addressed by would-be decipherers. Not only was it almost complete, but its cursive nature led some to suspect that it might be a more 'rational' script than the 'symbolic' hieroglyphic.*

C

The Greek text at the bottom of the Stone was easily readable. It thus provided the key that allowed the decipherment of the other two scripts.

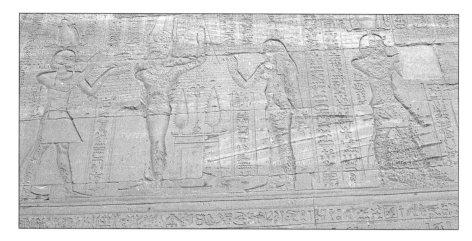

that alphabetic signs were used as such in ordinary narrative hieroglyphic script, despite the fact that a number of his existing transliterations pointed in this very direction.

The final resolution of the problem was therefore to be to the credit of Champollion, who had been working in parallel with Young. Like his British counterpart, Champollion had also been a child prodigy, who was learning both Hebrew and Arabic by the time he was 11 years old. Subsequently he learned Coptic at Grenoble, and obtained a university teaching post there at the tender age of 18. His formal career was much disrupted by his Republican political views, both under the late First Empire, and the Restoration monarchy in France after 1815. He obtained a Chair at Grenoble in 1818, but it was only in 1824 that he received official forgiveness from Louis XVIII, and the reward of a scientific mission to Italy to study Egyptian material there.

Champollion's first published contribution to the decipherment debate came in 1814, when he stated his view that Demotic and Coptic were the same language, differing only in the alphabets used. This conclusion was crucial, since it is a common (but not wholly true) axiom that an unknown language in an unknown script is undecipherable. Like Young, he also worked through many Book of the Dead manuscripts to establish equivalences between hieroglyphic and hieratic signs, but until 1820 was still tied to the idea that hieroglyphs were an entirely symbolic system, rather than having an alphabetic basis. Soon afterwards, however, he recanted, and embraced the theory that, for foreign names at least, hieroglyphs could be phonetic. Whether this was a result of having read Young's work, or arrived at independently, is still a hotly debated issue. Champollion certainly always claimed the latter; at this distance we shall never know.

Regardless of why he took the step, Champollion's recognition of the hieroglyphs' basic phonetic nature opened the way for rapid further progress. One useful experiment was to test Young's premise as to the relationship between the hieroglyphic, demotic, and hieratic scripts. Champollion experimentally worked backwards from the now long-established Demotic group for 'Ptolemy', and ultimately arrived at a group of hieroglyphs identical with that on the Rosetta Stone supposed to be that of Ptolemy. He tried this again with

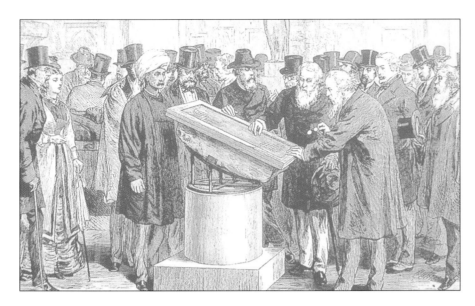

Left: The Rosetta Stone on display at the British Museum. The Museum took charge of the Rosetta Stone in June 1802, after its formal presentation by King George III. It has remained there on display ever since, except for a visit to Paris to mark the 150th anniversary of the decipherment.

Kleopatra, but was unable to check his result until a definite hieroglyphic writing of that queenly name was forthcoming.

THE STRONGMAN AND THE QUEEN

This was provided in 1821, with the arrival in England of an obelisk, removed from Philae by Giovanni Belzoni (1778–1823). A former circus strongman, he had first gone to Egypt as a hydraulic engineer. He subsequently undertook a series of commissions for Henry Salt (1780–1827), the British Consul in Egypt who, like his counterparts from the other European powers, was busy collecting antiquities on behalf of both his country and himself. Belzoni obtained a number of major monuments and opened a series of tombs, including the renowned sepulchre of Sethy I in the Valley of the Kings and the Second Pyramid at Giza. He also cleared a way into the Great Temple at Abu Simbel. Although often condemned as a plunderer, he took more care of his finds than most contemporaries, and published a comprehensive account of his work that was in many ways far ahead of its time. After leaving Egypt, he mounted an exhibition of his finds in Britain, and then went to explore west Africa; he died in Benin, en route to Timbuktu.

Following pages:
The gods Re-Harakhty and Osiris enthroned on a wall painting from Rameses I's tomb in the Valley of Kings. The splendour and mystery of Egyptian tombs and temples inspired generations of scholars to search for the meaning behind the fascinating enigma of hieroglyphic writing.

Left: Lunette of bilingual decree from Kom el-Hisn. The upper part of the Rosetta Stone is now lost; however, it most probably resembled that of this slightly earlier decree.

Above: *Thomas Young (1773–1829), one of the great polymaths of his age, made fundamental discoveries in the fields of medicine, physics and language. Although soon overtaken by Champollion, his work on papyri and the Rosetta Stone marked a quantum leap forward in the process leading to the final decipherment.*

Above: *Jean-François Champollion (1790–1832). The principal decipherer of hieroglyphs and the holder of the world's first university Chair of Egyptology.*

In 1816, William John Bankes (1786–1855) had discovered an obelisk outside the temple of the goddess Isis on the island of Philae. As usual, the obelisk itself bore texts in hieroglyphs, but its pedestal had a text in Greek. Belzoni was commissioned to bring the monument back to England, and it was ultimately erected in 1839 on Bankes' estate at Kingston Lacy, Dorset.

Bankes was a land-owner and Member of Parliament who travelled extensively in the Near East in 1815–19. He took a deep interest in Egyptian antiquities and followed the hieroglyphic debate. He took the view that the cartouches on the obelisk bore the same royal names (Ptolemy and Kleopatra) that appeared in Greek on the base, and made a similar observation regarding greek and hieroglyphic texts on the pylon of a now destroyed temple at Hu in Middle Egypt. However, he also believed (wrongly) that the hieroglyphic and greek texts on the obelisk were translations of each other, something also believed by Young and Consul Salt who, without much justification, fancied himself to be a hieroglyphic scholar.

With the availability of the Philae text, Champollion now had his two known cartouches. Both of them could be checked against their demotic versions, as well as against each other, since they belonged to individuals whose Greek names (Ptolemaios and Kleopatra) shared a number of letters. If hieroglyphs were indeed phonetic, their cartouches, and , should also share hieroglyphic signs. It was immediately apparent that the letters P, O and L were in their expected places: P⌂OL⌒ ⑂...; ⊿L⑂OP⬚⌒⌒⬚⌂○. With this taken as read, it was possible to identify most of the remaining signs: PTOLMEES; KLEOPA⌒RA⌂○. Given that the rest of the name was clearly that of Kleopatra, it was inevitable that ⌒ had to be something akin to 't' (it is actually a 'd'). The remaining ⌂○ had been observed by Young as following the signs which, by context, had to be feminine names. It was thus clear that it was a feminine ending, not meant to be read.

EXIT YOUNG

Champollion's basic approach had been very similar to that used by Young, working from greek and demotic names back to the hieroglyphic royal names, and thence to the values of the alphabetic signs, but with the important difference that most of his equivalences were correct. Nevertheless, Young had made important progress, which continued until he dropped active Egyptological work in 1823, following the publication of his *Account of some recent Discoveries in the Hieroglyphical Literature*. In doing so, he remarked that 'Champollion is doing so much that he will not suffer anything of material consequence to be lost'. Taking a sample of 14 signs, Young got five correct, and four partly correct; in contrast, 11 of Champollion's readings were right, and the remaining three partly so.

At the end of his initial work on the cartouches of Ptolemy and Kleopatra, Champollion had 13 alphabetic signs to work with. The cartouches of 'Alexander' and 'Berenike', together with certain early Roman emperors were rapidly identified, thus further adding to the number of known signs.

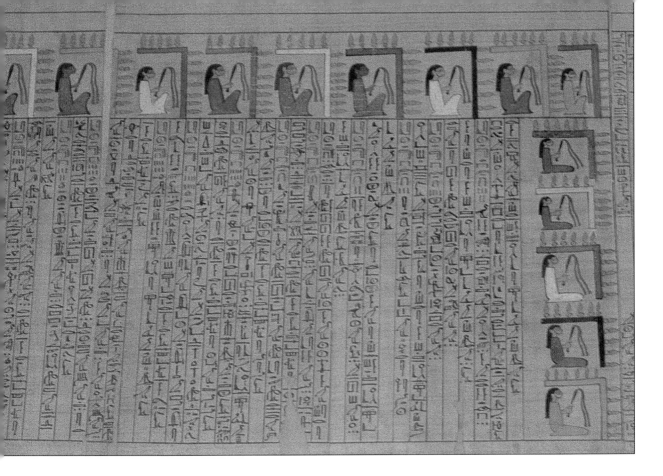

Above: *Anonymous copy of the Book of the Dead dating to the Third Intermediate Period. The main 'guidebook' to the afterlife is found in hundreds of copies, and in all three ancient Egyptian scripts: hieroglyphic, hieratic and demotic. Young and Champollion made considerable use of this to verify the way in which hieroglyphic signs related to their cursive equivalents.*

Having reached this point, Champollion was able to present his preliminary results in a famous communication to the French Académie des Inscriptions et Belles-Lettres ('the Academy') on 29 September 1822, the *Lettre à M. Dacier, relative à l'alphabet des hieroglyphes phonétiques* ('Letter to M. Dacier, regarding the phonetic hieroglyphic alphabet'). He still remained doubtful, however, as to whether all hieroglyphic texts were phonetic. It seemed possible that signs could have been adapted to write foreign names alphabetically in the Graeco-Roman Period, but were more normally employed in a symbolic fashion, which would mean that narratives and non-Greek names would still be a closed book. This was the same concern that had ultimately blocked Young from moving any further forward in his studies.

THE BREAKTHROUGH

It was therefore vital to test the theory against earlier, native, royal names. This was successfully carried out when, using the Coptic 're' for the sun sign in the cartouche (image), Champollion arrived at RE-?-SS ((image) had already been recognized as an epithet, meaning 'beloved of the god Amun', and not part of the actual name); there was also the cartouche (image), which Young had guessed might conceal the Greek 'Tuthmosis', which might be read as 'THOTH-?-S'. The king list written by the third-century BC Egyptian priest, Manetho strongly suggested that '?' should be 'm' or 'ms'. The Coptic link could once more be invoked, since the Greek word for 'to bear' apparently corresponded with (image) in the hieroglyphic text of the Rosetta Stone, and the Coptic for 'to bear' is 'mosi'. Champollion was thus able to read the purely

Egyptian names 'Rameses' and 'Thutmose', showing that the phonetic use of hieroglyphs was Egyptian practice, not simply that of later foreign conquerors.

Progress was then rapid. In 1824, Champollion published his *Précis du système hiéroglyphique* ('Summary of the hieroglyphic system'), and two years later was made Conservator of the Egyptian collection in the Louvre Museum in Paris. He undertook an expedition to Egypt in 1828–9, which built on the Napoleonic Commission's work to further enhance the documentation of the Egyptian monuments. His triumph was then capped by his appointment to the world's first full Professorship of Egyptology in March 1831. However, Champollion's constitution had been undermined by earlier experiences, and he died of a stroke only a year later.

While in Egypt, Champollion had met the Englishman John Gardner Wilkinson (1797–1875), who lived at Thebes from 1821 to 1833, studying the monuments and making a mass of notes and illustrations (now kept in Oxford University's Bodleian Library). With the vast amount of material of the Theban tombs and temples before him, Wilkinson was able to develop and correct a number of aspects of Champollion's work, in particular some of the latter's historical views. Knighted in 1839, he distilled his conclusions in a number of books, his great *Manners and Customs of the Ancient Egyptians* (1837) being the standard work for many decades; indeed, an abridged edition is still in print.

CHAMPOLLION'S LEGACY

At the time of Champollion's death, the manuscript of his *Grammaire Égyptienne* was complete, and was published in 1838. However, his remaining work was far from ready for publication and, worse, a number of items could not be found, including a large proportion of his projected dictionary. Luckily for Egyptology, Champollion's elder brother, Jacques-Joseph Champollion-Figeac (1778–1867) was zealous in placing his sibling's work before the world at large, following the government's purchase of his manuscripts in 1833. Thus, he piloted the *Grammaire* through the press, and began the publication of Jean-François' Egyptian expedition in 1835.

Champollion-Figeac's biggest problem, however, was the dictionary, of which about half the manuscript material had disappeared. He publicized the loss widely, in the hope that Jean-François had merely lent the papers to a colleague prior to his demise. Champollion-Figeac's suspicions were raised a year later, when he was sent a prospectus that described a three-volume work on the Rosetta Stone and Book of the Dead, to be published by one François

Above: *The island of Philae, as drawn by the French expedition, as it appears in* Commission des Monuments d'Egypte, *1809–22.*

Above: *Giovanni Battista Belzoni (1778–1823), adventurer, explorer and excavator.*

Opposite: *The First Pylon of the Temple of Isis, Philae. Two obelisks flanking the approach were erected by Ptolemy VIII Euergetes II and Kleopatra III.*

Above: *The Bankes Obelisk, now in the grounds of Kingston Lacy House, Dorset. It had been found by the Temple of Isis at Philae, by William John Bankes and taken to England some 20 years after its discovery.*

Above: *Gustavus Seyffarth (1796–1885), the longest lived of Champollion's opponents. His 'system' embraced various bizarre concepts, which produced 'translations' that bore little resemblance to the true meaning of texts. Nevertheless, he did useful work, most importantly making the first reconstruction of the Canon of Kings in Turin.*

Salvolini, a 22-year-old former student of the younger Champollion, who had been studying Egyptology for only a year.

At meeting of the Academy in August 1833, Silvestre de Sacy, who had also been Champollion's mentor, appealed for information on the lost manuscripts' whereabouts – to which Salvolini added his own tearful appeal; nothing was then heard for seven years. Then, Charles Lenormant (1802–59), one of Champollion's former collaborators, was approached by Luigi Verardi, who was attempting to wind up the affairs of Salvolini, who had died tragically young in 1838. Verardi had been trying, with very little success, to sell a series of manuscripts bearing Salvolini's name, and was seeking advice on how to proceed. As soon as Lenormant saw these manuscripts, it was clear to him that the lost writings of Champollion had been found. Confronted by this fact, Verardi agreed to sell Salvolini's archive to Lenormant for 600 French francs, the Champollion material joining the rest of his material under Champollion-Figeac's editorial pen.

The *Dictionnaire* was published in 1841, but suffered from its words being arranged by the kind of thing represented by their initial sign, rather than alphabetically. The decision to do so had been taken by Champollion-Figeac, since his brother had not had time to undertake any kind of arrangement before his death. In addition, the hieroglyphs had been transcribed into coptic letters, with an underlying assumption that all words written in hieroglyphs would correspond to ones in Coptic – which was not the case (*see Chapter II*). There was a more fundamental problem in that Champollion had never grasped the difference between uniliteral, biliteral and triliteral signs, believing, for example, that (m), (mr), (mi), (mn), (ms), were all simply 'm'; this multiplication of signs with allegedly the same reading had been a major cause for disquiet amongst those opposing Champollion's system. Finally, many of Champollion's conclusions were presented only in provisional form; there remained many gaps and inconsistencies, and clearly very much more work was required before it would be possible to read a connected ancient Egyptian narrative without recourse to a bilingual text such as the Rosetta Stone.

The pretenders

Considerable time elapsed before the whole of the orientalist world was able to accept that Champollion had indeed identified the correct system for deciphering the hieroglyphs. During the 13 years that followed the first appearance of the 1824 *Précis*, opponents of Champollion's conclusions included I.A. Goulianov (1784–1841), Heinrich Klaproth (1783–1835), Cataldi Janelli (*fl.* 1830), Francesco Ricardi (*fl.* 1821–43) and Friedrich Spohn (1792–1824). A number of these presented more-or-less misguided alternative approaches, one of the longest lived being that developed by Spohn and Gustavus Seyffarth (1796–1885).

In 1830, Seyffarth received the first Professorship in Archaeology at Leipzig University, but the hieroglyphic system he embraced suffered from a fundamental problem: no two users seemed able to produce the same translation of a given text – not surprisingly, given that a single sign could apparently have a up to a dozen different values, depending on context!

Ultimately, he emigrated to America in 1854 against the background of the wholesale rejection of his philological theories in his native Germany. Nevertheless, his researches had important practical results, including in 1826 the first reconstruction of the the great King List from the myriad papyrus fragments in Turin. Seyffarth's misfortune was to cling to his erroneous hypotheses long beyond the point at which Champollion's correct one had started to prove itself, even into the phase during which it had received universal acceptance. By the early 1860s, he had only one disciple left, Max Uhlemann, who himself died in 1862; however, Seyffarth still felt sufficiently sure of himself that year to engage in vitriolic exchange in print with the British Egyptologist, Sir Peter Le Page Renouf (1822–97), who had had the temerity to point out the main flaws in Seyffarth's theories. Seyffarth maintained his position until his death, aged 91, in 1885, a tragic loss to the true study of Egyptian.

Above: *Carl Richard Lepsius (1810–84). In addition to his great contribution to the study of the Egyptian language, Lepsius led the Prussian expedition to Egypt in 1842–5, whose discoveries and records remain fundamental. From 1864 he was Professor of Egyptology at Berlin and in 1866 discovered a complete copy of the Decree of Canopus at Tanis.*

THE END OF THE MYSTERY

The death-knell to these alternate theories of decipherment had already come in 1837, when the Prussian Egyptologist Carl Richard Lepsius (1810–84) produced his *Lettre à M. le Professeur H. Rosellini sur l'Alphabet Hiéroglyphique* (Letter to Professor H. Rossellini about the Hieroglyohic Alphabet). Having undertaken a systematic comparison of all the various proposed methods of

Left: *The Great Temple of Rameses II at Abu Simbel in Nubia, which provided the cartouche of Rameses II that so helped Champollion. The area south of Aswan also contains some of the very last hieroglyphic inscriptions ever made in Egypt.*

Tableau des Signes Phonétiques des Écritures hiéroglyphique et Démotique des anciens Égyptiens

Lettres Grecques	Signes Démotiques	Signes Hiéroglyphiques
A		
B		
Γ		
Δ		
E		
Z		
H		
Θ		
I		
K		
Λ		
M		
N		
Ξ		
O		
Π		
P		
Σ		
T		
Υ		
Φ		
Ψ		
X		
Ω		
ΤΟ. ΤΩ.		

Above: A page from Champollion's Lettre à M. Dacier, *in which he compares Greek, Demotic and Hieroglyphic signs.*

decipherment, he was able to show that Champollion's was certainly the correct one, although not without its problems. These he undertook to correct, for example those regarding the existence of signs that represented more than one letter, and the true relationship between Coptic and the more ancient versions of the language. Thirty years later, Lepsius discovered a copy of another trilingual text, the Decree of Canopus, that allowed scholars to verify the conclusions of Champollion and his successors.

In England, Samuel Birch (1813–85), from 1836 of the British Museum, was also involved in widening and deepening Champollion's system. He had previously studied Chinese and, unlike earlier writers such as de Guignes and Palin who had misused the similarities between the Chinese and Egyptian scripts (*see previous chapter*), made good use of his knowledge in the classification of Egyptian words. The dictionary which he began to prepare was based on Chinese phonetic classification principles, and drew on all Egyptian material in the museum, together with all the words in the texts published by James Burton (1788–1862), John Gardiner Wilkinson (1797–1875), Ippolito Rosellini (1800–43), Champollion and Salvolini. In 1838, Birch published a sampler for the proposed dictionary, containing 12 pages with 93 words; unfortunately, there was insufficient interest to allow the publication of the whole book to go ahead. It was not until nearly 30 years later that Birch's dictionary would finally appear.

Meanwhile, in Ireland, Edward Hincks (1792–1866) was engaged in important work on both hieroglyphs and the Mesopotamian cuneiform script, being both dubbed the 'founder of Assyrian grammar', and described as the first person to correctly transliterate Egyptian texts, and to fully recognize the language's Semitic characteristics. In France, Champollion's mantle had now been picked up by Emmanuel de Rougé (1811–72), and by the 1850s he was able to read running texts, something no previous worker had been able to do. He was a key figure in the recognition of the earlier phases of the language, in particular Old Egyptian, through his production of the first translation of the Sixth Dynasty inscription of Uni. This important work had hitherto been regarded as too difficult. De Rougé's career culminated in his assumption of Champollion's Chair at the Collège de France in Paris in 1860, where he taught many of the next generation of Egyptologists. His pupil, Gaston Maspero (1846–1916) summarized the relative achievements of Champollion and de Rougé as follows: 'Champollion deciphered the texts .... De Rougé gave us the method which allowed us to utilize and bring to perfection the discovery of Champollion'.

THE END OF THE BEGINNING

De Rougé's work marked the end of the formative phase of the study of Egyptian. Although texts could now be read for the first time since the Roman Period,

Below: Champollion's Dictionnaire was arranged by his brother according to the items that the first sign of a word represented. Thus, ♀ (ḥr) and ⊕ (tp) are together; in a modern dictionary, the words shown here are placed far apart, under their initial letters. Like many dictionaries of ancient Egyptian, the text was handwritten and lithographed, owing to the problems with typesetting hieroglyphs.

Above: *Samuel Birch (1813–85) worked in the Public Records Office before moving to the British Museum in 1836. The pivotal British figure in establishing the correctness of Champollion's decipherment, he was much in demand as a lecturer, as well as writing for both the academic and popular audience.*

many areas of obscurity remained, some of which have still not been properly resolved. Throughout the middle years of the nineteenth century, scholars such as de Rougé, Birch, Lepsius, Heinrich Brugsch (1827–94), Charles Goodwin (1817–78) and François Chabas (1817–82) laboured to resolve problems. Birch's long-planned *Dictionary* was finally published in 1867, although unfortunately 'hidden' as the fifth volume of a multi-volume history of Egypt. Even more unfortunately, it rapidly went out of print, and in the 1870s, the budding Egyptologist Wallis Budge (1857–1934) was forced to trace his own copy of it – all 612 pages! The same year (1867), Brugsch brought out his hieroglyphic-demotic dictionary, a vast work of 759 pages and some 5,000 words, plus a supplement of similar length.

The production of these great volumes was the culmination of what has been termed the 'lexicographical' phase of the study of ancient Egyptian. Since Young and Champollion's day, the focus of studies had been on the decipherment and collection of words. Although there had, of course, been work on the grammar that glued them all together, quite rightly the priority was to find out the basic meanings of the signs and groups of signs. However, from the 1870s onwards, the focus began to switch, particularly through the work of a group of young German scholars based in Berlin – the so-called 'Berlin School'. The leading member of this grouping was Adolf Erman (1854–1937), whose works, together with those of his students and associates, revolutionized the whole study of the language.

THE BERLIN SCHOOL

Erman was the first worker to fully understand the differences between the different phases of Egyptian – Old, Middle and Late – and also the way it fitted into its family of languages. His volume on Late Egyptian grammar was issued in 1880, the same year as his fellow Berliner, Ludwig Stern (1846–1911), produced his important Coptic grammar. Stern, however, abandoned the subject in 1884 on Erman's appointment as head of the Egyptian Department at the Berlin Museum, the Coptic mantle in Berlin being picked up by Georg Steindorff (1861–1951), who had been Erman's first student. The 'Berlin School' triumvirate was completed by Kurt Sethe (1869–1934), another student of Erman's, who later was to become Professor at Göttingen University.

The Berlin School was especially concerned with the way that Egyptian grammar operated, particularly with reference to the verb. They attempted to put linguistic study on a fully systematic basis, one example being their promotion of the method of transliteration that is largely still being used today. In the latter part of the nineteenth century, a wide range of methods was used to transcribe Egyptian scripts into roman letters. A long drawn out discussion of transliteration methods was to be found in the various Egyptological and archaeological journals, from which the 'Berlin method' ultimately emerged victorious. Nevertheless, some scholars refused to accept the 'new' method, and some of the old approaches were still to be found down to the 1930s, particularly in the works of French Egyptologists and in the writings of the British scholar Wallis Budge.

The other legacy of the Berlin school is the greatest of all hieroglyphic dictionaries, the *Wörterbuch der ägyptischen Sprache* ('Dictionary of the Egyptian Language'), begun in 1897 and edited by Erman and Hermann Grapow (1885–1967). The latter was yet another student of Erman and Steindorff, upon whom almost all the work gradually devolved after World War I. Comprising 11 folio volumes, the material was compiled by a commission on which many of the leading Egyptologists of the day served. As with most such enterprises, the words and their references were collected on slips of paper, known as '*Zettel*', and aimed to include all known inscriptions and manuscripts. In the end, over 1,500,000 slips were compiled. The published text was handwritten and lithographed, six volumes being written out by the Danish Egyptologist, Wolja Erichsen (1890–1966). The *Wörterbuch* remains the fundamental reference work of its kind, although supplemented by various one-volume dictionaries, the most widely used one into the English language being *A Concise Dictionary of Middle Egyptian* (1962), by Raymond Faulkner (1894–1982) of University College London.

One of those who accepted many of the Berlin findings was Francis Llewellyn Griffith (1862–1934), the first great British philologist since the death of Birch. As the first Professor of Egyptology at Oxford University he laid the foundations for that institution's own 'school', of whom the key figures were Sir Alan Gardiner (1879–1963) and Battiscombe Gunn (1883–1950). Gardiner had studied under Erman, and did a vast amount of work on the translation and publication of texts, testing out the syntax lying behind them while doing so. A major fruit of this work is his *Egyptian Grammar*, first published in 1927, and still in print three-quarters of a century later. Intended as a teaching tool, the vast majority of today's English speaking Egyptologists first learned their hieroglyphs from it and, although new teaching grammars are now appearing, modern students are still experiencing its 31 lessons.

Gunn, Griffith's successor in the Oxford Chair, published relatively little, a situation to which his extremely high standards contributed much. Nevertheless, his *Studies in the Egyptian Syntax* (1924) broke new ground in the study

Right: A column from Samuel Birch's dictionary, published in 1867. It was the first to use a hieroglyphic font, made especially for his work, and was the first complete Egyptian dictionary to be issued, and listed some 9,270 words.

I. Alphabet phonétique général

1.	2.	3.	4.	5.	6.	7.	8.	9.	10.	11.	12.	13.	14.	15.

II. Signes devenus phonétiques au commencement de certains groupes.

Above: Lepsius' breakthrough: the Egyptian phonetic alphabet confirmed in his Lettre ... Rosellini.

of the verb, and compressed a vast amount of material into a compact form. Another key British figure was Walter Crum (1865–1944), a Berlin-trained Copticist, assessed as the equal of only Steindorff in modern studies of the last phase of the Egyptian language. His greatest monument is his *Coptic Dictionary* (1929–39), a 1,000-page tome that was published in spite of the author having to abandon many of his materials in Vienna, when caught there by the outbreak of World War I.

MODERN TIMES

The work of the Berlin School and its immediate successors brought Egyptian philological studies to a level at which they remained until after World War II. It was then that the work of Hans Jakob Polotsky (1905–91) came under consideration. Yet another product of Berlin, as well as Göttingen, Polotsky's work on aspects of the Coptic and Egyptian syntax led to a revolutionary reconsideration of key aspects of the underlying structure of the language.

His work has been a point of departure for many of the more recent scholars of the language, concerned not so much with the words and grammar, but with the fundamentals of *why* meanings are as they are, rather than simply *what* a given passage means. Some of Polotsky's conclusions, such as the nature of Egyptian verbal forms, are now being challenged by such scholars as Mark Collier of the University of Liverpool, but his standing is without question.

The ongoing debate on this and many other issues is an indication both of the health of Egyptian philology as a subject, and the fact that, much as we now know about the ancient language of Egypt, that knowledge is still incomplete. As new texts are discovered, areas of uncertainty can be resolved, but it is certain that some obscure texts will remain so, particularly those dealing with religious concepts that may have been somewhat opaque to the majority of the ancients themselves! As well as this refinement of our knowledge of the mature language, important research is revealing evidence for the very earliest years of the hieroglyphic script's life. While the 'mystery' of the

Above: *Francis Llewellyn Griffith (1862–1934), the first Professor of Egyptology at Oxford University. For years Britain's foremost Egyptian philologist, he did much important work in publishing texts.*

In addition, he performed the feat of deciphering the Sudanese Meroitic script, although the actual language written still remains largely obscure. Meroitic is written in a script ultimately derived from hieroglyphs, but is unrelated linguistically to ancient Egyptian.

Left: *A page from the great Berlin Wörterbuch, showing its inclusion of meanings, together with variant writings. It was the culmination of Egyptian lexicography.*

THE TANIS STELA

On 15th April 1866, four researchers – Carl Lepsius, Maximilian Weidenbach, Leo Reinisch and Robert Roessler – were visiting the site of ancient Tanis when they stumbled across the corner of a stone projecting from the debris near some fallen obelisks. This had been spotted earlier, but ignored, by an engineer working on the nearby Suez Canal. It was a stela inscribed with a decree containing almost perfect hieroglyphic and greek versions of the same text. It was not until two years after its discovery that Heinrich Brugsch realized that some 'scratches' on the left-hand edge of the stela were actually the demotic version of the text! The Tanis Decree offered confirmation of the theories put forward on the basis of the Rosetta Stone.

THE FACE OF THE TANIS DECREE

FALLEN OBELISKS AT SAN EL-HAGAR, ANCIENT TANIS

hieroglyphs is no more, there will long be material to keep researchers occupied just as intensively as were the founding fathers of hieroglyphic studies.

Knowledge of the ancient script is also now more widespread than at any time since the Greco-Roman times. Universities all over the world teach the language, while adult education classes in the subject remain extremely popular. As recently as 1998, a self-teaching guide (Collier and Manley's *How to Read Egyptian Hieroglyphs*) became an unexpected best-seller in the United Kingdom, an eloquent testimony to the attractions of an Egyptian culture that has been dead for nearly two millennia.

The study of hieroglyphs and the language they enshrine has moved from the first fumbling attempts to isolate the significance of individual signs, to the situation today where the minutiae of the language are being investigated to the same degree as any other language. Ancient Egyptian texts are no longer 'deciphered' – they are simply 'read', but this position has only been reached as the result of the labours of many individuals over nearly four centuries. Without such scholars as Kircher, Young, Champollion, de Rougé and Erman, the hieroglyphs might still hold their mystery.

Opposite: King Sethy I before the god Anubis, in the king's temple at Abydos.

Left: Sir Alan Gardiner whose Egyptian Grammar was for over 50 years the text book most commonly used by students of ancient Egyptian.

DYNASTIES AND CHRONOLOGIES

ROYAL NAMES ARE TO BE FOUND on a wide variety of ancient Egyptian monuments, from tombs and temples to obelisks. As we have seen in Chapter II, a monarch had up to five 'great names', but they were seldom all found used together. While the preferred name(s) varied with time, it is the cartouche-names – the nomen and prenomen – which are most frequently seen.

While the spellings seen in them were fairly standard down to the New Kingdom, from the Nineteenth Dynasty onwards, there was an increasing variety of ways in which a given king's name could be written. At worst, there can be 20 or more ways of writing a given cartouche, although normally there are only two or three regularly found variants. In some cases this reflected the

fact that a given king used a number of different epithets to add to his basic names (*see pages 26–27*). In other cases, it was simply that a range of spellings or arrangements of signs were used to write the same name.

The latter often explains the differences between cartouches when written vertically, as against horizontally. The Egyptian scribe was usually keen to ensure that the most aesthetic arrangement of signs was used, even if this meant placing them out of their logical order. Thus it is frequently almost impossible to decipher such a royal name from first principles, without fairly extensive background knowledge.

In the following tables, the most common or characteristic forms are given, although it should be noted that in the Roman Period the variety of spellings increases to such an extent that it is difficult to pin down a single writing. Readers interested in a comprehensive listing of known royal names should consult the *Handbuch der ägyptische Königsnamen* (*The Handbook of Egyptian King-Names*), von Beckerath, 1984/1999).

THE HIEROGLYPHIC NAMES OF THE KINGS OF EGYPT

The lists below give the hieroglyphic forms of the principal names of some of the more important kings. Some rulers used a wide variety of spellings; this list attempts to give the most characteristic or straightforward version.

DYNASTY I

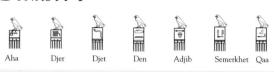

Aha   Djer   Djet   Den   Adjib   Semerkhet   Qaa

DYNASTY II

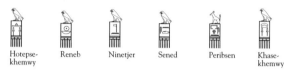

Hotepse-khemwy   Reneb   Ninetjer   Sened   Peribsen   Khase-khemwy

DYNASTY III

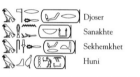

Djoser
Sanakhte
Sekhemkhet
Huni

DYNASTY IV

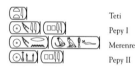

Seneferu
Khufu
Djedefre
Khaefre
Menkaure
Shepseskaf

DYNASTY V

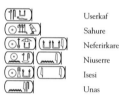

Userkaf
Sahure
Neferirkare
Niuserre
Isesi
Unas

DYNASTY VI

Teti
Pepy I
Merenre
Pepy II

DYNASTY XI

Inyotef II
Montjuhotpe II
Montjuhotpe III

DYNASTY XII

Amenemhat I
Senwosret I
Amenemhat II
Senwosret II
Senwosret III
Amenemhat III
Amenemhat IV
Sobkneferu

DYNASTY XIII

Sobkhotpe I
Amenemhat V
Qemau
Amenemhat VI
Sinedjhiryotef

Sobkhotpe II
Hor
Amenemhat VII
Wegaf
Khendjer
Imyromesho
Inyotef IV
Seth (y)
Sobkhotpe III
Neferhotep I
Sobkhotpe IV
Sobkhotpe V
Sobkhotpe VI
Iaib
Aya

DYNASTY XV

Khyan
Apopi

DYNASTY XVI

Djehuty
Nebiriau I

DYNASTY XVII

Rahotpe
Sobkemsaf I
Inyotef V
Inyotef VI
Sobkemsaf II
Taa II
Kamose

DYNASTY XVIII

Ahmose
Amenhotep I
Thutmose I
Thutmose II
Thutmose III
Hatshepsut
Amenhotep II
Thutmose IV
Amenhotep III
Akhenaten
Neferneferuaten
Tutankhamun
Ay
Horemheb

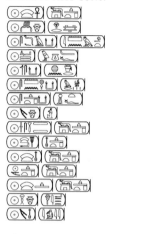

DYNASTY XIX

Rameses I

Sethy I

Rameses II

Merenptah

Sethy II

Amenmesse

Siptah

Tawosret

DYNASTY XX

Sethnakhte

Rameses III

Rameses IV

Rameses V Amenhirkopshef I

Rameses VI Amenhirkopshef II

Rameses VII Itamun

Rameses VIII Sethhirkopshef

Rameses IX Khaemwaset I

Rameses X Amenhirkopshef III

Rameses XI Khaemwaset II

DYNASTY XXI

Nesibanebdjed

Pinudjem I

Pasebkhanu I

Amenemopet

Osorkon the Elder

Siamun

Pasebkhanu II

DYNASTY XXII

Shoshenq I

Osorkon I

Takelot I

Osorkon II

Shoshenq III

Shoshenq IV

Pimay

Shoshenq V

Pedubast II

Osorkon IV

DYNASTY XXIII

Harsiese

Takelot II

Pedubast I

Osorkon III

Takelot III

Rudamun

Peftjauawybast

DYNASTY XXIV

Tefnakhte

Bakenrenef

DYNASTY XXV

Pi(ankh)y

Shabaka

Shabataka

Taharqa

Tanutamun

DYNASTY XXVI

Psametik I

Nekau II

Psametik II

Wahibre

Ahmose II

Psametik III

DYNASTY XXVII

Kambyses

Darios I

Xerxes I

Artaxerxes I

DYNASTY XXVIII

Amenirdis

DYNASTY XXIX

Nayfarud I

Pashhermut

Hakar

DYNASTY XXX

Nakhtnebef

Djedhor

Nakhthorheb

DYNASTY OF MACEDONIA

Alexander III

Philippos Arrhidaeos

Alexander IV

DYNASTY OF PTOLEMY

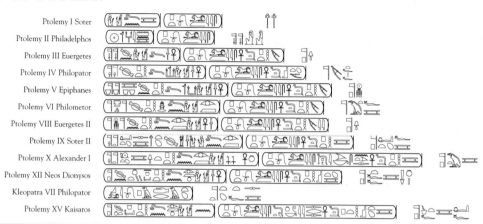

Ptolemy I Soter	
Ptolemy II Philadelphos	
Ptolemy III Euergetes	
Ptolemy IV Philopator	
Ptolemy V Epiphanes	
Ptolemy VI Philometor	
Ptolemy VIII Euergetes II	
Ptolemy IX Soter II	
Ptolemy X Alexander I	
Ptolemy XII Neos Dionysos	
Kleopatra VII Philopator	
Ptolemy XV Kaisaros	

ROMAN EMPERORS: PRENOMINA

Autokrator   Kaisaros   Autokrator Kaisaros

JULIO-CLAUDIAN DYNASTY

Augustus
Tiberius
Caligula
Claudius
Nero

FLAVIAN DYNASTY

Vespasian
Titus
Dominitian

CHRONOLOGY AND THE KINGS OF ANCIENT EGYPT

A Note on Egyptian Chronology

The scheme used by modern scholars for structuring the chronology of historic ancient Egypt is based upon one drawn up by the Egyptian priest, Manetho, around 300 BC. He divided the succession of kings into a series of numbered 'dynasties', corresponding to our idea of royal 'houses' (e.g. Plantagenet, Windsor, Bourbon, Hapsburg, Hohenzollern). These broadly fit in with our knowledge of changes in the ruling family, but in some cases the reason for a shift is unclear.

Historians of ancient Egypt have refined this structure by grouping dynasties into 'Kingdoms' and 'Periods', during which constant socio-political themes can be identified.

Ancient dating was by means of regnal years, rather than the kind of 'era' dating used today (e.g. BC, AD and AH). Thus, absolute dates, in terms of years BC, have to be established through various indirect methods. Some reigns can be fixed by relation to events linked to better-dated cultures, while others can be placed by reference to mentions of various astronomical phenomena. These allow other reigns' extent to be calculated by dead-reck-

oning. Nevertheless, there remain many areas of uncertainty and, while dating is solid back to 663 BC, margins of error before then may run in excess of century.

Another area of uncertainty is caused by the fact that a number of kings were crowned in advance of their fathers' deaths, to serve as their co-regents; in some cases they died before the elder king. In most, but not all cases, the younger king employed his own regnal years in parallel with those of the senior monarch. During the Middle Kingdom we have a few double-dates, which allow us to work out how the two dating systems relate to one another. However, the majority of co-regencies lack such guides, and in at least one case debate still rages over whether a co-regency lasted one or twelve years. As much of Egyptian chronology is based on the counting back of known regnal years from a fixed point, such uncertainties magnify the existing problems.

NB. Parentheses indicate co-ruler only

PREDYNASTIC PERIOD

Badarian Culture	5000-4000 BC
Naqada I (Amratian) Culture	4000-3500 BC
Naqada II (Gerzian) Culture	3500-3150 BC

PROTODYNASTIC PERIOD
Naqada III Culture   3150–3000 BC

HORUS OR THRONE NAME	PERSONAL NAME	CONJECTURAL DATES	REGNAL YEARS
ARCHAIC PERIOD			
Dynasty I			
Horus Narmer		3050–	
Horus Aha		:	
Horus Djer	Itit	:	
Horus Djet	Iti	:	
Horus Den	Semti	:	
Horus Adjib	Merpibia	:	
Horus Semerkhet	Irinetjer	:	
Horus Qaa	Qebh	–2813	
Dynasty II			
Horus Hotepsekhemwy	Baunetjer	2813–	
Horus Nebre	Kakau	:	
Horus Ninetjer	Ninetjer	:	
?	Weneg	:	
?	Sened	:	
Horus Sekhemib/ Seth Peribsen	Peribsen	:	
?	Neferkare	–2709	
?	Neferkasokar	2709–2701	8
?	?	2701–2690	11
Horus and Seth Khasekhemwy	Nebwyhetepimyef	2690–2663	27
OLD KINGDOM			
Dynasty III			
Horus Netjerkhet	Djoser	2663–2643	19
Horus Sanakht	Nebka	2643–2633	9
Horus Sekhemkhet	Djoser-ti	2633–2626	6
Horus Khaba	Teti?	2626–2621	6
Horus Qahedjet?	Huni	2621–2597	24
Dynasty IV			
Horus Nebmaet	Seneferu	2597–2547	50
Horus Medjedu	Khufu	2547–2524	23
Horus Kheper	Djedefre	2524–2516	8
Horus Userib	Khaefre	2516–2493	23
Horus Kakhet	Menkaure	2493–2475	18
Horus Shepseskhet	Shepseskaf	2475–2471	4
Dynasty V			
Horus Irimaet	Userkaf	2471–2464	7
Horus Nebkhau	Sahure	2464–2452	12
Neferirkare	Kakai	2452–2442	10
Shepseskare	Isi	2442–2435	7
Horus Neferkhau	Neferefre	2435–2432	3
Niuserre	Ini	2432–2421	11
Menkauhor	Ikauhor	2421–2413	8
Djedkare	Isesi	2413–2385	28
Horus Wadjtawy	Unas	2385–2355	30
Dynasty VI			
Horus Seheteptawy	Teti	2355–2343	12
Nefersahor/Meryre	Pepy I	2343–2297	46
Merenre	Nemtyemsaf I	2297–2290	7
Neferkare	Pepy II	2290–2196	94
Merenre?	Nemtyemsaf II	2196–2195	1
FIRST INTERMEDIATE PERIOD			
Dynasty VII/VIII			
Netjerkare	?	2195–	
Menkare?	Nitokris	:	
Neferkare	?	:	
Neferkare	Neby	:	
Djedkare	Shemay	:	
Neferkare	Khendu	:	
Merenhor	?	:	
Nikare	?	:	
Neferkare	Tereru	:	

HORUS OR THRONE NAME	PERSONAL NAME	CONJECTURAL DATES	REGNAL YEARS
Neferkahor	?	:	
Neferkare	Pepysonbe	:	
Neferkamin	Anu	:	
Qakare	Ibi	:	4
Wadjkare	?	:	
Neferkauhor	Khuihapy	:	
Neferirkare	?	–2160	
Dynasties IX/X			
Meryibre	Akhtoy I	2160–	
Neferkare	?	:	
Wahkare	Akhtoy II	:	
?	Senenen ...	:	
Neferkare	Akhtoy III	:	
Mery...	Akhtoy IV	:	
(Various)	(Various)	:	
?	Meryhathor	:	
Nebkaure	Akhtoy V	:	
Merykare	?	:	
?	?	–2040	
Dynasty XIa			
Horus Tepya	Montjuhotpe I	2160–	
Horus Sehertawy	Inyotef I	–2123	
Horus Wahankh	Inyotef II	2123–2074	49
Horus Nakhtnebtepnefer	Inyotef III	2074–2066	8
MIDDLE KINGDOM			
Dynasty XIb			
Nebhepetre	Montjuhotpe II	2066–2014	52
Sankhkare	Montjuhotpe III	2014–2001	13
Nebtawyre	Montjuhotpe IV	2001–1994	7
Dynasty XII			
Sehetepibre	Amenemhat I	1994–1964	30
Kheperkare	Senwosret I	1974–1929	45
Nubkhaure	Amenemhat II	1932–1896	36
Khakheperre	Senwosret II	1900–1880	20
Khakaure	Senwosret III	1881–1840	41
Nimaetre	Amenemhat III	1842–1794	48
Maekherure	Amenemhat IV	1798–1785	13
Sobkkare	Sobkneferu	1785–1781	4
Dynasty XIII			
Sekhemre–khutawi	Sobkhotpe I	1781–	3
Sekhemkare	Sonbef	:	3
Nerikare	?	:	1
Sekhemkare	Amenemhat V	:	3
Sehetepibre	Qemau	:	2
Sankhibre	Amenemhat VI	:	
Smenkare	Nebnuni	:	
?	Iufeni	:	
Hotepibre	Sihornedjhiryotef	:	
Swadjkare	?	:	
Nedjemibre	?	:	
Khaankhre	Sobkhotpe II	:	
Sekhemre-khutawi	Renisonbe	:	
Auibre	Hor	:	
Sedjefakare	Amenemhat VII	:	
Khutawire	Wegaf	:	
Userkare/ Nikhanimaetre	Khendjer	:	
Smenkhkare	Imyromesha	:	
Sehotepkare	Inyotef IV	:	
Meryibre	Seth(y)	:	
Sekhemre-swadjtawi	Sobkhotpe III	:	3
Khasekhemre	Neferhotpe I	:	11
Menwadjre	Sihathor	:	
Khaneferre	Sobkhotpe IV	:	
Merhotepre	Sobkhotpe V	:	
Khahetepre	Sobkhotpe VI	:	4
Wahibre	Iaib	:	10
Merneferre	Aya	:	23
Merhetepre	Ini	:	2

HORUS OR THRONE NAME	PERSONAL NAME	CONJECTURAL DATES	REGNAL YEARS
Sankhenre	Sewadjtu		
Mersekhemre	Ined		
Sewadjkare	Hori		
Merkaure	Sobkhotpe VII	:	
Mershepsesre	Ini	:	
Mersekhemre	Neferhotpe II	:	
[5 unknown kings]		:	
Mer[...]re	?	:	
Merkheperre	?	:	
Merkare	?	:	
?		:	
Sewadjare	Montjuhotpe V	:	
[...]mesre	?	:	
[...]maetre	Ibi	:	
[...]webenre	Hor[..]	:	
Se[...]kare	?	:	
Seheqaenre	Sankhptahi	:	
Sekhaenre	[...]s	:	
Sewahenre	Senebmiu	–1650	

SECOND INTERMEDIATE PERIOD

Dynasty XV

HORUS OR THRONE NAME	PERSONAL NAME	CONJECTURAL DATES	REGNAL YEARS
	Semqen?	1650–	
	Sakirhar	:	
Seuserenre	Khyan	:	
Nebkhepeshre/ Aqenenre/Auserre	Apopi	1585–1545	40
?	Khamudy	1545–1535	

Dynasty XVI

HORUS OR THRONE NAME	PERSONAL NAME	CONJECTURAL DATES	REGNAL YEARS
?	?	1650–	
Sekhemre-smentawi	Djehuty	:	
Sekhemre-sewosertawi	Sobkhotpe VIII	:	
Sekhemre-seankhtawi	Neferhotpe III	:	
Sankhenre	Montjuhotepi	:	
Swadjenre	Nebiriau I	:	
Neferkare?	Nebiriau II	:	
Semenre	?	:	
Seuserenre	Bebiankh	:	
Sekhemreshedwaset	?	:	
Djedhotepre	Dedumose I	:	
Djedneferre	Dedumose II	:	
Djedankhre	Montjuemsaf	:	
Merankhre	Montjuhotpe VI	:	
Seneferibre	Senwosret IV	1590	

Dynasty XVII

HORUS OR THRONE NAME	PERSONAL NAME	CONJECTURAL DATES	REGNAL YEARS
Sekhemre-wahkhau	Rehotpe	1585–	
Sekhemre-shedtawi	Sobkemsaf I	:	
Sekhemre-wepmaet	Inyotef V	:	
Nubkheperre	Inyotef VI	:	
Sekhemre-heruhirmaet	Inyotef VII	:	
Sekhemre-wadjkhau	Sobkemsaf II	:	
Senakhtenre	Taa I	1558–	
Seqenenre	Taa II	1558–1553	5
Wadjkheperre	Kamose	1553–1549	4

NEW KINGDOM
Dynasty XVIII

HORUS OR THRONE NAME	PERSONAL NAME	CONJECTURAL DATES	REGNAL YEARS
Nebpehtire	Ahmose I	1549–1524	25
Djeserkare	Amenhotep I	1524–1503	21
Akheperkare	Thutmose I	1503–1491	12
Akheperenre	Thutmose II	1491–1479	12
Menkheper(en)re	Thutmose III	1479–1424	54
(Maetkare	Hatshepsut	1472–1457)	
Akheperure	Amenhotep II	1424–1398	26
Menkheperure	Thutmose IV	1398–1388	10
Nebmaetre	Amenhotep III	1388–1348	40
Neferkheperure-waenre	Amenhotep IV/ Akhenaten	1360–1343	17
(Ankhkheperure	Smenkhkare/ Neferneferuaten	1346–1343	3)
Nebkheperre	Tutankhamun	1343–1333	10
Kheperkheperure	Ay	1333–1328	5
Djeserkheperure-setpenre	Horemheb	1328–1298	30

Dynasty XIX

HORUS OR THRONE NAME	PERSONAL NAME	CONJECTURAL DATES	REGNAL YEARS
Menpehtire	Rameses I	1298–1296	2
Menmaetre	Sethy I	1296–1279	17
Usermaetre-setpenre	Rameses II	1279–1212	67
Banenre	Merenptah	1212–1201	11
Userkheperure	Sethy II	1201–1195	6
(Menmire-setpenre	Amenmesse	1200–1196	4)
Sekhaenre/Akheperre	Siptah	1195–1189	6
Sitre-merenamun	Tawosret	1189–1187	2

Dynasty XX

HORUS OR THRONE NAME	PERSONAL NAME	CONJECTURAL DATES	REGNAL YEARS
Userkhaure	Sethnakhte	1187–1185	2
Usermaetre-meryamun	Rameses III	1185–1153	32
User/Heqamaetre-setpenamun	Rameses IV	1153–1146	7
Usermaetre-sekheperenre	Rameses V Amenhirkopshef I	1146–1141	5
Nebmaetre-meryamun	Rameses VI Amenhirkopshef II	1141–1133	8
Usermaetre-setpenre-meryamun	Rameses VII Itamun	1133–1125	8
Usermaetre-akhenamun	Rameses VIII Sethhirkopshef	1125–1123	2
Neferkare-setpenre	Rameses IX Khaemwaset I	1123–1104	19
Khepermaetre-setpenre	Rameses X Amenhirkopshef III	1104–1094	10
Menmaetre-setpenptah	Rameses XI Khaemwaset II	1094–1064	30
(Hemnetjertepyenamun	Hrihor	1075–1069	6)

THIRD INTERMEDIATE PERIOD

Dynasty XXI

HORUS OR THRONE NAME	PERSONAL NAME	CONJECTURAL DATES	REGNAL YEARS
Hedjkheperre-setpenre	Nesibanebdjed	1064–1038	26
Neferkare-heqawaset	Amenemnesu	1038–1034	4
(Kheperkhare-setpenamun	Pinudjem I	1049–1026	23)
Akheperre-setpenamun	Pasebkhanu I	1034–981	53
Usermaetre-setpenamun	Amenemopet	984–974	10
Akheperre-setpenre	Osorkon the Elder	974–968	6
Netjerkheperre-meryamun	Siamun	968–948	20
(Tyetkheperure-setpenre	Pasebkhanu II	945–940)	

Dynasty XXII

HORUS OR THRONE NAME	PERSONAL NAME	CONJECTURAL DATES	REGNAL YEARS
Hedjkheperre-setpenre	Shoshenq I	948–927	21
Sekhemkheperre-setpenre	Osorkon I	927–892	35
(Heqakheperre-setpenre	Shoshenq II	895–895)	
Hedjkheprre-setpenre	Takelot I	892–877	15
Usermaetre-setpenamun	Osorkon II	877–838	39
Usermaetre-setpenre	Shoshenq III	838–798	40
Hedjkheperre-setpenre	Shoshenq IV	798–786	12
Usermaetre-setpenamun	Pimay	786–780	6
Akheperre	Shoshenq V	780–743	37
Sehetepibenre	Pedubast II	743–733	10
Akheperre-setpenamun	Osorkon IV	733–715	18

Dynasty XXIII

HORUS OR THRONE NAME	PERSONAL NAME	CONJECTURAL DATES	REGNAL YEARS
Hedjkheperre-setpenamun	Harsiese	867–857	10
Hedjkheperre-setpenre	Takelot II	841–815	26
Usermaetre-setpenamun	Pedubast I	830–799	30
(?	Iuput I	815–813)	
Usermaetre-setpenamun	Osorkon III	799–769	30
Usermaetre	Takelot III	774–759	15
Usermaetre-setpenamun	Rudamun	759–739	20
	Iny	739–734	5
Neferkare	Peftjauawybast	734–724	10

Dynasty XXIV

HORUS OR THRONE NAME	PERSONAL NAME	CONJECTURAL DATES	REGNAL YEARS
Shepsesre	Tefnakhte	731–723	8
Wahkare	Bakenrenef	723–717	6

Dynasty XXV

HORUS OR THRONE NAME	PERSONAL NAME	CONJECTURAL DATES	REGNAL YEARS
Seneferre	Pi(ankh)y	752–717	35
Neferkare	Shabaka	717–703	14

HORUS OR THRONE NAME	PERSONAL NAME	CONJECTURAL DATES	REGNAL YEARS
Djedkare	Shabataka	703–690	13
Khunefertumre	Taharqa	690–664	26
Bakare	Tanutamun	664–656	8

SAITE PERIOD

Dynasty XXVI
Wahibre	Psametik I	664–610	54
Wehemibre	Nekau II	610–595	15
Neferibre	Psametik II	595–589	6
Haaibre	Wahibre	589–570	19
Khnemibre	Ahmose II	570–526	44
Ankhka(en)re	Psametik III	526–525	1

LATE PERIOD

Dynasty XXVII
Mesutire	Kambyses (Kembitjet)	525–522	3
Setutre	Darios I (Intiryosh)	521–486	35
?	Xerxes I (Khashyarsha)	486–465	21
?	Artaxerxes I (Artakheshes)	465–424	41
?	Xerxes II	424	1
?	Darios II	423–405	18

Dynasty XXVIII
?	Amenirdis	404–399	5

Dynasty XXIX
Baenre-merynetjeru	Nayfarud I	399–393	6
Userre-setpenptah	Pashermut	393	1
Khnemmaetre	Hakar	393–380	13
?	Nayfarud II	380	1

Dynasty XXX
Kheperkare	Nakhtnebef	380–362	18
Irimaetenre	Teos	362–360	2
Senedjemibre-setpenanhur	Nakhthorheb	360–342	18

Dynasty XXXI
	Artaxerxes III Okhos	342–338	5
	Arses	338–336	2
	Darios III	335–332	3

HELLENISTIC PERIOD

Dynasty of Macedonia
Setpenre-meryamun	Alexander III	332–323	9
Setepkaenre-meryamun	Philippos Arrhidaeos	323–317	5
Haaibre	Alexander IV	317–310	7

Dynasty of Ptolemy
Setpenre-meryamun	Ptolemy I Soter	310–282	28
Userka(en)re-meryamun	Ptolemy II Philadelphos	285–246	36
Iwaennetjerwysenwy-setpenre-sekhemankhen-amun	Ptolemy III Euergetes I	246–222	24
Iwaennetjerwymenek-hwysetpenptah-userkare-sekhemankhenamun	Ptolemy IV Philopator	222–205	17
Iwaennetjerwy-merwyyot-setpenptah-userkare-sekhemankhenamun	Ptolemy V Epiphanes	205–180	25
Iwaennetjerwyperwy-setpenptahkhepri-irimaetamunre	Ptolemy VI Philometor	180–164	16
Iwaennetjerwyperwy-setpenptah-irimaetre-sekhemankenamun	Ptolemy VIII Euergetes II	170–163	7
	Ptolemy VI (again)	163–145	18
?	Ptolemy VII Neos Philopator	145	1
	Ptolemy VIII (again)	145–116	29

HORUS OR THRONE NAME	PERSONAL NAME	CONJECTURAL DATES	REGNAL YEARS
Iwaennetjermenekhnet-jeretmerymutesnedjet-sepenptah-merymaetre-sekhemankhamun	Ptolemy IX Soter II	116–110	6
Iwaennetjermenekh-netjeretmenekhsatre-setpenptah-irimaetre-senenankhenamun	Ptolemy X Alexander I	110–109	1
	Ptolemy IX (again)	109–107	2
	Ptolemy X (again)	107–88	19
	Ptolemy IX (again)	88–80	8
(?	Ptolemy XI	80	1)
Iwaenpanetjerentine-hem-setpenptah-mery maetenresekhemankh amun	Ptolemy XII Neos Dionysos	80–58	22
	Ptolemy XII (again)	55–51	4
	Kleopatra VII Philopator	51–30	21
(?	Ptolemy XIII	51–57	4)
(?	Ptolemy XIV	47–44	3)
(Iwaenpanetjerentinehem-setpenptah-irimeryre-sekhemankhamun	Ptolemy XV Kaisaros	41–30	11)

ROMAN PERIOD	BC 30–395 AD
BYZANTINE PERIOD	395–640
ARAB PERIOD	640–1517
OTTOMAN PERIOD	1517–1805
KHEDEVAL PERIOD	1805–1914
BRITISH PROTECTORATE	1914–1922
MONARCHY	1922–1953
REPUBLIC	1953–

Alternate forms of Pharaoh's names

As mentioned in Chapter I, there are various ways of transcribing royal names, both based on the original Egyptian, and using the Greek forms used by Classical authors. Some of the most common equivalences are given below:

Horus Narmer	Menes
Khufu	Kheops
Khaefre	Khephren, Rekhaef
Menkaure	Mycerinus
Amenemhat	Ammenemes
Senwosret	Sesostris, Senusert
Ahmose	Amosis, Amasis
Amenhotep	Amenophis
Thutmose	Tuthmosis
Sethy	Sethos, Seti
Nesibanebdjed	Smendes
Pasebkhanu	Psusennes
Bakenrenef	Bokkhoris
Wahibre	Apries
Nayfarud	Nepherites
Pashermut	Teos
Hakar	Akhoris
Nakhtnebef	Nektanebo I
Nakhthorheb	Nektanebo II

WHERE TO SEE HIEROGLYPHS

*Egyptian collections are to be found all around the world.
This list gives a selection of some of the more important
collections, particularly those rich in inscribed items.*

AUSTRIA
VIENNA Kunsthistorisches Museum

BELGIUM
BRUSSELS Musées Royaux d'Art et d'Histoire

CANADA
TORONTO Royal Ontario Museum

DENMARK
COPENHAGEN Nationalmuseet
COPENHAGEN Ny Carlsberg Glyptotek

EGYPT
ALEXANDRIA Greco-Roman Museum
ASWAN Nubian Museum
CAIRO Egyptian Museum
LUXOR Luxor Museum
PORT SAID Port Said Museum

ENGLAND
BIRMINGHAM City Museums and Art Gallery
BOLTON Museum and Art Gallery
BRISTOL City Museum and Art Gallery
CAMBRIDGE Fitzwilliam Museum

THE SECOND PYRAMID AT GIZA

DURHAM Oriental Museum
ETON Myers Collection, Eton College
EXETER Royal Albert Museum
LIVERPOOL Liverpool Museum
LONDON British Museum
LONDON Petrie Museum of Egyptian Archaeology,
  University College
MANCHESTER Manchester Museum
NORWICH Castle Museum
OXFORD Ashmolean Museum
TRURO Royal Cornwall Museum

FRANCE
MARSEILLE Musée d'Archéologie Mediterranéenne
PARIS Musée du Louvre

GERMANY
BERLIN Ägyptisches Museum un Papyrussammlung
HANOVER Kestner-Museum
HEIDELBERG Sammlung des Ägyptologischen Instituts
  der Universität
HILDESHEIM Pelizaeus-Museum
LEIPZIG Ägyptischen Museum der Universität
MUNICH Staatliche Sammlung Ägyptischer Kunst
TUBINGEN Ägyptische Sammlung der Universität

HUNGARY
BUDAPEST Szépmüvészeti Múzeum

IRELAND
DUBLIN National Museum

ITALY
BOLOGNA Museo Civico Archeologico
FLORENCE Museo Egizio
MILAN Civiche Raccolte Archeologiche e
  Numismatiche
PISA Collezioni Egittologiche di Ateneo
TURIN Museo Egizio

NETHERLANDS
AMSTERDAM Allard Pierson Museum
LEIDEN Rijksmuseum van Oedheden

POLAND
WARSAW Museum Narodowe

THE VALLEY OF THE KINGS

RUSSIA
MOSCOW State Pushkin Museum of Fine Arts
ST PETERSBURG Hermitage Museum

SCOTLAND
ABERDEEN Marischel Museum
EDINBURGH Royal Museum
GLASGOW Burrell Collection
GLASGOW Hunterian Museum

SPAIN
BARCELONA Museu Egyipci de Barcleona
MADRID Museo Arqueológico Nacional

SWEDEN
STOCKHOLM Medelhavsmuseet
UPPSALA Victoriamuseet

SWITZERLAND
BASEL Antikenmuseum Basel und Sammlung Ludwig
GENEVA Musée d'art et d'histoire

THUTMOSE III ON THE VII PYLON AT KARNAK

'FECUNDITY FIGURE' IN THE TEMPLE OF RAMESES II AT ABYDOS

UNITED STATES OF AMERICA
ANN ARBOR, MI Kelsey Museum of Ancient and
  Medieval Archaeology
ATLANTA, GA Michael C. Carlos Museum, Emory
  University
BALTIMORE, MD Walters Art Gallery
BOSTON, MA Museum of Fine Arts
BROOKLYN, NY Brooklyn Museum of Art
CHICAGO, IL Art Institute
CHICAGO, IL Field Museum of Natural History
CHICAGO, IL Oriental Institute Museum
CLEVELAND, OH Cleveland Museum of Art
DETROIT, MI Detroit Institute of Arts
LOS ANGELES, CA County Museum of Art
MEMPHIS, TN Institute of Egyptian Art and
  Archaeology, Memphis University
NEWARK, NJ Newark Museum
NEW HAVEN, CT Peabody Museum, Yale University
NEW YORK, NY Metropolitan Museum of Art
PHILADELPHIA, PA University Museum of Archaeology
  & Anthropology
SAN JOSE, CA Rosicrucian Egyptian Museum

VATICAN
VATICAN CITY Museo Gregoriano Egizio

WALES
SWANSEA Egypt Centre, University of Wales Swansea

GLOSSARY

biliteral hieroglyphic sign representing combination of two consonants

Book of the Dead compilation of texts and images intended to facilitate the movement of the dead person's spirit to the next world

cartouche oval enclosure with flat bar at one end, enclosing the king's prenomen and nomen; sometimes used for queens and royal children, and also for gods in the Greco-Roman Period

Coffin Texts set of religious texts originally inscribed on the interior of coffins of the Middle Kingdom

consonant letter other than a vowel

Coptic final variant of the ancient Egyptian language, written in a script largely composed of greek letters, with admixture of some demotic, known as coptic

cursive writing done without lifting the pen between letters

demotic cursive script derived from hieratic, introduced during Dynasty XXV

Demotic the variant of the ancient Egyptian language written in the demotic script

determinative hieroglyphic sign that usually has no phonetic value, but indicates the general meaning of group of signs that precede it

epithet word or collection of words that describes or characterizes a noun or a name

'Golden falcon' name third name of the royal five-fold titulary, of obscure significance

hieratic cursive script derived from hieroglyphs, introduced during the Old Kingdom

hieroglyph figure of object standing for sound or word

DYNASTY V SCRIBE AT WORK

Horus name first name of the royal five-fold titulary, written in a serekh and associating the ruler with the falcon-god, Horus

Late Egyptian the version of the ancient Egyptian language first used for written documents in the New Kingdom

lexicography the making of dictionaries

Middle Egyptian the version of the ancient Egyptian language in general use during the Middle Kingdom and retained as a literary form, especially for religious texts, until the Roman Period

Nebty name second name of the royal five-fold titulary, associating the ruler with the two goddesses, Edjo and Nekhbet

nomen fifth name of the royal five-fold titulary, written in a cartouche, and often preceded by the title 'son of the sun-god'

noun word used as name of person or thing

Old Egyptian the version of the ancient Egyptian language used during the Old Kingdom

ordinal roman numeral placed after the name of a monarch to distinguish them from earlier bearers of the same name; e.g. George V, George VI

papyrus paper manufactured from the pith of the papyrus plant

Pharaoh Biblical version of the Egyptian phrase pr-ꜥ3, 'great house'; originally referred to the palace, but from the New Kingdom was used as a title for the king; occasionally found written in a cartouche in the Greco-Roman Period

philology the science of the study of language

phonetic of or representing vocal sound

prenomen fourth name of the royal five-fold titulary, written in a cartouche, and preceded by a title that emphasizes the kingships dual aspect

pronoun word serving as substitute for a noun

Pyramid Texts set of religious texts originally inscribed on the walls of the passages and chambers of the pyramids of the Old Kingdom

serekh rectangular frame with panelled lower part, usually surmounted by an image of the falcon-god Horus, and enclosing the king's Horus-name

titulary combination of titles used by kings and officials.

transliteration the direct conversion of hieroglyphic, hieratic or demotic texts into the roman (western) alphabet

triliteral hieroglyphic sign representing combination of three consonants

uniliteral hieroglyphic sign representing single consonants

verb part of speech expressing action, occurence or being

vernacular speech in common use

ABBREVIATIONS

BM British Museum, London.
BMA Brooklyn Museum of Art
CM Egyptian Museum, Cairo
EAE *Encyclopedia of the Archaeology of Ancient Egypt*, ed. by K.A. Bard (London: Routledge, 1999)
GI Griffith Institute, Ashmolean Museum, University of Oxford
ILN *Illustrated London News* (London)

JE Journal d'Entrée (CM)
JEA *Journal of Egyptian Archaeology* (London)
KMT: *A Modern Journal of Egyptology* (San Francisco/Sebastopol)
MFA Museum of Fine Arts, Boston
MMA Metropolitan Museum of Art, New York
RMS Royal Museum of Scotland

SR Special Register (CM)
TR Temporary Register (CM)
TSBA *Transactions of the Society of Biblical Archaeology* (London)
TT Theban Tomb (the numbering system used for private tomb-chapels)
UC Petrie Museum, University College London

BIBLIOGRAPHY AND WEBSITES

GENERAL

ALDRED, C. 1998. *The Egyptians*, 3rd edition, revised by A. Dodson (London: Thames and Hudson)
DAVIS, W.V. 1987. *Egyptian Hieroglyphs* (London: British Museum Press)
DODSON, A. 1996/2001. *Monarchs of the Nile* (London: Rubicon Press/Cairo: American University in Cairo Press)
KEMP, B.J. 1989. *Ancient Egypt: Anatomy of a Civilisation* (London: Routledge)
MANLEY, B. 1996. *The Penguin Historical Atlas of Ancient Egypt* (London: Penguin, 1996)
REDFORD, D.B. 2001. (ed.) *The Oxford Encyclopedia of Ancient Egypt* (New York: Oxford University Press)
SHAW, I. (Ed) 2000. *The Oxford History of Ancient Egypt* (Oxford: Oxford University Press)

CHAPTER I: THE ORIGINS OF EGYPTIAN LANGUAGE

BAINES, J. & J. MALEK 1980. *Atlas of Ancient Egypt* (New York and Oxford: Facts on File)

MOST ANCIENT EGYPT

ADAMS, B. 1995. *Ancient Nekhen: Garstang in the City of Hierakonpolis* (New Malden: Sia Publishing)
HOFFMAN, M.A. 1980. *Egypt Before the Pharaohs* (London: Routledge and Kegan Paul)
MIDANT-REYNES, B. 2000. *The Prehistory of Egypt* (Oxford: Blackwell)

THE DAWN OF WRITING

BAINES, J. 1989. 'Commununication and display: the integration of early Egyptian art and writing', *Antiquity* 63: 471–82
BAINES, J. 1999. 'Writing, invention and early development', *EAE*, 882–5
DAVIS, W. 1992. *Masking the Blow: The Scene of Representation in Late Prehistoric Egyptian Art* (Berkeley: University of Californian Press)
DREYER, G. 1998. *Umm el-Qaab I. Das prädynastische Königsgrab U-j und seine frühen Schriftzeugnisse* (Mainz: Philipp von Zabern)
DREYER, G. 1999. 'Abydos Umm el-Qa'ab', *EAE*: 109–14
RAY, J.D. 1986. 'The Emergence of Writing in Egypt', *World Archaeology* 17/3: 307–16

EGYPTIAN NAMES AND TITLES

BECKERATH, J. von 1984/1999. *Handbuch der ägyptischen Königsnamen* (Munich: Deutscher Kunstverlag/Mainz: Philipp von Zabern)
QUIRKE, S. 1990. *Who were the Pharaohs?* (London: British Museum Press)

CHAPTER II: THE ANCIENT EGYPTIAN LANGUAGE

ALLEN, J.P. 2000. *Middle Egyptian: An Introduction to the Language and Culture of Hieroglyphs* (Cambridge: Cambridge University Press)
COLLIER, M. and B. MANLEY 1998. *How to Read Egyptian Hieroglyphs* (London: British Museum Press)
DEPUYOT, L. 1999. *Fundamentals of Egyptian Grammar* (Part I: *Elements*) (Norton/Merken: Frog Publishing)

ERMAN, A. and H. GRAPOW 1926–31. *Wörterbuch der ägyptischen Sprache*, 5vv (Leipzig: Heinrichs')
GARDINER, Sir A. 1957. *Egyptian Grammar: being an introduction to the study of hieroglyphs*, 3rd edition (Oxford: Griffith Institute)
FAULKNER, R.O. 1962. *A Concise Dictionary of Middle Egyptian* (Oxford: Griffith Institute)
GELB, I.J. 1963. *A Study of Writing*, rev. edn. (Chicago: Chicago University Press)
LOPRIENO, A. 1995. *Ancient Egyptian: A Linguistic Introduction* (Cambridge: Cambridge University Press).
MÖLLER, G. 1909–12. *Hieratische Paläographie* (Leipzig: Heinrichs)
THOMPSON, S.E. 1999. 'Egyptian language and writing', *EAE*: 274–7

CHAPTER III: THREE MILLENNIA OF WRITING

BAINES, J.R. 1983. 'Literacy and Ancient Egyptian Society', *Man* 18: 572-99
CERNY, J. 1952. *Paper and books in Ancient Egypt* (London: H.K. Lewis, reprinted Chicago: Ares Press)
DAVIES, N.M. 1958. *Picture Writing in Ancient Egypt* (Oxford: Oxford University Press)
GOEDICKE, H. 1972. 'Hieroglyphic Inscriptions of the Old Kingdom', in *Textes et languages de'Égypte pharaonique. Cent cinquante ans de recherches (1822-1972). Hommage à J.-F. Champollion* (Cairo: IFAO): 16–24.
HARRIS, J.R. (ed.) 1971. *The Legacy of Egypt* (Oxford: Clarendon Press).

JAMES, T.G.H., 1984. *Pharaoh's People* (London: Bodley Head; New York: Oxford University Press)

LICHTHEIM, M. 1975–80. *Ancient Egyptian Literature*, 3vv (Berkeley: University of California Press)

MERTZ, B. 1978. *Red Land, Black Land* (New York: Dodd, Mead & Co.)

PARKINSON, R.B., 1991. *Voices from Ancient Egypt* (London: British Museum Press)

SCHÄFER, H. 1974. *Principles of Egyptian Art* (Oxford: Oxford University Press)

SIMPSON, W.K. (ed.) 1972. *The Literature of Ancient Egypt* (New Haven and London: Yale University Press)

SMITH, W.S., 1998. *The Art and Architecture of Ancient Egypt*, rev by W.K. Simpson (New Haven: Yale University Press)

WILKINSON, R.H. 1994. *Symbol and Magic in Egyptian Art* (London: Thames and Hudson)

INSCRIPTIONS FOR THE GODS

SCHAFER, B.E. (ed.) 1997. *Temples of Ancient Egypt* (London: I.B. Tauris)

SCHWALLER DE LUBCZ, R.A. 1999. *The Temples of Karnak* (London: Thames and Hudson)

THE TEXTS OF BURIAL

DODSON, A. and S. IKRAM 2004. *The Tomb in Ancient Egypt* (London: Thames & Hudson)

FAULKNER, R.O. 1969. *The Ancient Egyptian Pyramid Texts* (Oxford: University Press)

FAULKNER, R.O. 1994. *The Egyptian Book of the Dead* (San Francisco: Chronicle Books)

HORNUNG, E. 1990. *The Valley of the Kings: Horizon of Eternity* (New York: Timken Publishers)

HORNUNG, E., 1999. *The Ancient Egyptian Books of the Afterlife* (Ithaca & London: Cornell University Press)

IKRAM, S. and A. DODSON 1998. *The Mummy in Ancient Egypt* (London: Thames and Hudson)

SPENCER, J. 1982. *Death in Ancient Egypt* (Harmondsworth: Penguin)

HISTORICAL INSCRIPTIONS

BREASTED, J.H. 1905. *Ancient Records of Egypt*, 5vv (Chicago: Chicago University Press; reprinted London:

Histories and Mysteries of Man, 1988)

CHRONICLES

REDFORD, D.B. 1986. *Pharaonic King-Lists, Annals and Day-Books* (Mississauga: Benben)

EXPEDITION RECORDS

ALBRIGHT, W.F. 1966. *The Proto-Sinaitic Inscriptions and their Decipherment* (Cambridge MA: Harvard University Press)

GARDINER, A.H. 1916. 'The Egyptian Origin of the Semitic Alphabet', *JEA* 3: 1–16

TEXTS OF MAGIC AND MEDICINE

NUNN, J.F. 1996. *Ancient Egyptian Medicine* (London: British Museum Press)

CHAPTER IV: THE MYSTERY OF THE HIEROGLYPHS

HORAPOLLO 1993. The *Hieroglyphics of Horapollo*, translated and introduced by G. Boas (Princeton: University Press)

IVERSEN, E. 1961/1993. *The Myth of Egypt and Its Hieroglyphs in European Tradition* (Copenhagen: Gadd/Princeton: University Press)

CHAPTER V: DECIPHERMENT OF HIEROGLYPHS

ADKINS, L. and R. 2000. *The Keys of Egypt: The Race to Read the Hieroglyphs.* (London: HarperCollins)

ANDREWS, C. 1981. *The Rosetta Stone* (London: British Museum Press)

BUDGE, E.A.W. 1893. 'Memoir of Samuel Birch', *TSBA* 9: 1–43

BUDGE, E.A.W. 1904. *The Decrees of Mamphis and Canopus*, 3vv (London: Kegan Paul, Trench, Trübner)

BUDGE, E.A.W. 1920. *An Egyptian Hieroglyphic Dictionary*, I (London: John Murray): v–lxxiv

BUDGE, E.A.W. 1925. 'The Decipherment of the Egyptian Hieroglyphs', in *The Mummy* (Cambridge: University Press): 123–64

COMMISSION DES MONUMENTS D'ÉGYPTE 1809–22. *Description de l'Égypte, ou Recueil des observations et des recherches qui ont été faites en Égypte pendent l'expédition de l'armée français: Antiquités* (Planches), 9 + 10vv (Paris: Imprimerie impériale)

DAWSON, W.R. 1958. 'The Discoverer

of the Rosetta Stone: a Correction', *JEA* 44: 123

DAWSON, W.R. and E.P. UPHILL 1995. *Who Was Who in Egyptology*, 3rd edition by M.L. Bierbrier (London: Egypt Exploration Society)

DEPUYOT, L. 1999. 'Egyptian (language), decipherment of', *EAE*: 271–4

GRIFFITH, F.LI. 1951. 'The Decipherment of the Hieroglyphs', *JEA* 37: 38–46

HALL, H.R. 1916. 'Letters of Champollion le Jeune and of Seyffarth to Sir William Gell', *JEA* 2: 76–87

IVERSEN, E. 1972. 'The Bankes Obelisk', in *Obelisks in Exile*, II (Copenhagen: Gadd): 62–85

KAMAL, A. 1904–5. *Stèles ptolémaiques et romaines* (Cairo: Institut français d'archéologie orientale)

MAYES, S. 1959. *The Great Belzoni* (London)

PARKINSON, R. 1999. *Cracking Codes: the Rosetta Stone and Decipherment* (London: British Museum Press)

POPE, M. 1999. *The Story of Decipherment, from Egyptian Hieroglyyphs to Maya Script*, revised edition (London: Thames & Hudson)

RENOUF, Sir P. Le Page 1859. 'Seyffarth and Uhleman on Egyptian Hieroglyphics', *Atlantis* 1859, II/3: 74–97, reprinted in G. Maspero and W.H Rylands (eds), *The Life Work of Sir Peter Le Page Renouf I* (Paris: Ernest Leroux, 1902): 1–31

RENOUF, Sir P. 1862. 'Dr Seyffarth and the Atlantis on Egyptology' *Atlantis* III/6: 306–38, reprinted in *Life Work*: 33–80

SIMPSON, R.S. 1996. *Demotic Grammar in the Ptolemaic Sacerdotal Decrees* (Oxford: Griffith Institute)

VERCOUTTER, J. 1992. *The Search for Ancient Egypt* (London: Thames & Hudson)

USEFUL WEBSITES

http://www.newton.cam.ac.uk/egypt/index.html

http://www.breakingthecode.com

http://www.fnspo.cz/mmm/egypt/hiero/1.htm

http://www.quizland.com/hiero.htm

INDEX

A

abbreviations 139
Abercromby, Sir Ralph 106
Abu Simbel 17, 111
Abusir 60, 70, 72, 76
Abydos
  festival of Osiris 68–9
  king-lists 74
  royal tombs 11, 15, 17, 23
  temple of Rameses II 34–5, 75
  temple of Sethy I 76, 86, 99, 127
Account of some recent Discoveries in the Hieroglyphical Literature 112
adjectives 49
administrative documents 76–7
agriculture 12–13, 14, 30, 52
Ahmose I 70
Ahmose II 45
Ahmose-Pennekhbet 70
Ahmose-si-Ibana 66–7, 70
Åkerblad, Johan David 109
Alexander the Great 26, 90, 94
Alexander, hieroglyph 112
alphabet 38–41, 124
Amenemhab, General 70
Amenemhat I 69
Amenemhat II 61
Amenemhat III 14
Amenemhat V 27
Amenemhat VI 27
Amenemhat, Vizier 78
Amenemsaf, papyrus of 65
Amenhirkopshef, Prince 29
Amenhotep II 26
Amenhotep III 26, 33, 63
Amenhotep IV 26
Amenmesse 18, 76
Ameny-Qemau 27
Ammanius Marcellinus 96
Ammenemes I 69
Amratian culture
  see Naqada I
Amun, god 26, 31
Amun-Re, temple of 31, 72
ancient Egyptian names 31, 33
Anhurkhau 82–3
Ankheshoshenq, Instructions of 80
Ankhnespepy, Queen 74
Anubis, god 36, 127
Arab Period 95, 97, 135
Arabic 36, 92, 97, 109
Archaic period 11, 36, 58, 133
Aswan 17, 68, 69, 78, 98, 100

Asyut 45, 71
autobiographies 66–71

B

Badarian Period 10, 14
Bakenkhonsu, high priest 30
Bankes, William John 105, 112, 118
Barthélemy, Abbé Jean Jacques 102, 103, 104
Belzoni, Giovanni Battista 111, 112, 115
Beni Hasan, tomb 3 54
Berinike, hieroglyph 107, 112
Berlin school 122–4
biliterals 44, 118
biographies 58
Birch, Samuel 121, 122, 123
bird gods 24, 28, 32, 44
'The Blinding Truth by Falsehood' 87
boat imagery 15
Bonaparte, Napoleon 104, 106
Book of Coming Forth by Day (*see* Book of the Dead)
Book of the Dead
  chronology 59
  decipherment aid 107, 110, 113, 115
  function 64, 65, 138
  hieratic script 47
Bouchard, Pierre-François-Xavier 106
British Museum 106, 121, 136
Brugsch, Heinrich 122, 127
Budge, Wallis 122
Burton, James 121
Butehamun, scribe 85
Byzantine Period 37, 94, 135

C

calendar 52
Canon of Kings 122
Canopus, Decree of 90, 110, 119, 121, 127
cartouche 24, 26, 27, 28, 128, 138
Chabas, François 122
Chairemon 96
Champollion, Jean-François 105–7, 110–11, 112–15, 118, 121
Champollion-Figeac, Jacques-Joseph 115, 118
Chancellor 30, 87
Christianity 46, 51, 90, 94–6, 97
chronicles 74–5
chronology 132–5
civil war 21, 59, 61, 63, 71

Claudius 27, 132
Clement of Alexandria 96
climate changes 14
Coffin Texts 58, 59, 64, 138
Collier, Mark 124
Colonna, Francesco 99
common names 33
consonants 42, 44, 138
Coptic
  decipherment aid 110, 113, 120–1
  definition 138
  dictionary 124
  grammar 122, 124
  language/development 36, 37, 46, 47, 51
  reinterpretation 99–100
Coptic Period 37, 94, 135
court proceedings 76, 77
Crum, Walter 124
cults 31, 63, 68, 99
cursive script 45, 102, 138

D

Dahshur 14, 60
dates 52–3, 132
de Guignes, Joseph 102–3
de Rougé, Emmanuel 121, 122
de Sacy, Baron Antoine-Silvestre 109, 118
death *see* funerary
decipherment of hieroglyphs
  Berlin school 122–4
  breakthrough 112–15, 119–22
  chronology 104–5
  modern debate 124–6
  phonetic theory 110, 113, 115
  rediscovery/interpretation 92, 96–103
  Rosetta Stone 47, 90, 104–9
  theories 109–19
decrees
  bilingual 111
  Canopus 90, 110, 119, 121, 127
  chronology 58
Deir el-Bahari 79, 85, 98
Deir el-Medina 76, 77, 82–3, 85
della Valle, Pietro 99
demotic script 138
  deciphering 106, 107, 109, 112, 127
  development 37, 51
  last use 104
  uses 45, 47, 90
Den, tomb of 25
Dendara 99

Description de l'Egypte 104, 106
determinatives 42–4, 102, 138
development of hieroglyphs 8–9, 10, 15, 17, 36
Dictionary (Birch) 121, 122, 123
Dictionary, Coptic (Crum) 124
Dictionary of the Egyptian Language (Berlin school) 123, 125
Dictionnaire (Champollion) 118, 121
Diodorus Siculus 94
Divine Legation of Moses, The 102
Djed, god 33
Djet, tomb of 24
Djhutmose, scribe 45, 85
Djoser, King 59
Domitian 27, 100, 102, 103
Duamutef 65

E

Edfu, temple 32, 63
Edjo, goddess 23
Edwin Smith Surgical Papyrus 88
Egypt
  Champollion's expedition 115
  civil war 21, 59, 61, 63, 71
  decline in power 73, 90, 94–5
  foundation 10–11, 14, 20
  geography 10–12
  geology 14, 17
  monarchy 135
  Napoleonic expedition 104, 106
  Prussian expedition 119
  Republic 135
  unification 11, 20
  as world power 68, 72
Egyptian collections 136–7
Egyptian Grammar 123
Egyptology, first professorship 115
El-Amra 14
El-Kab 66–7, 70
Elephantine Island 17
epithets 26–7, 28, 33, 113, 128, 138
Erichsen, Wolja 123
Erman, Adolf 122, 123
expedition records 78–9

F

Farouq, King 93
fathers, names 27, 29

Faulkner, Raymond 123
Fayoum cultures 14
filiative nomina 27, 29
First Intermediate Period 36, 58, 133
Flavian dynasty 132
Fort Julien 106, 107
France
  Champollion's expedition 115
  Napoleonic expedition 104, 106
  Professorship of Egyptology 115
funerary books 47, 59, 64–5
funerary chapels 64, 65
funerary domains 30
funerary inscriptions 60, 62, 63, 64

G
Gardiner, Sir Alan 123, 127
Gebel el-Silsila 14
Gerzean culture
  see Naqada II
Giza 11, 60, 65, 92, 93, 111
glossary 138
gold 24
Golden Falcon name 24, 27, 56, 138
Goodwin, Charles 122
Goulianov, I.A. 118
graffiti 90
Grammaire Égyptienne 115
grammar 48–9, 122, 123–4, 127
Grapow, Hermann 123
Greek names 22
greek script
  Coptic basis 47
  decipherment aid 47, 96, 112
  language impact 37, 45, 59, 90, 94
  Rosetta Stone 47, 106, 107, 109
Griffith, Francis Llewellyn 123, 125
Gunn, Battiscombe 123

H
hand-written texts 45, 47, 58, 102, 138
Hapy, god 12, 65
Harkhuf 68, 78
Harpers Songs 80–1
Hathor, goddess 27
Hatshepsut 32, 81, 98, 105
heart 65
Hebrew 109
Heliopolis 98
Hellenistic Period 135
Hemaka, tomb 61
Heqanakhte, priest 85

Hermapion 96
Hermes 96
Hermetic Corpus 96, 101
Hierakonpolis 14, 20
hieratic script 138
  Coffin Texts 58
  in columns 85
  deciphering 102, 107
  decline 90
  hieroglyphic equivalents 40–2, 102
  uses 45, 47, 58, 90
Hieroglyphica 96–7, 99
hieroglyphs
  see also decipherment of hieroglyphs
  alphabet 38–41, 124
  decline 90, 92, 94, 96
  definition 138
  development 8–9, 10, 15, 17, 36
  direction 103
  early examples 10, 15, 17, 20–1
  first 10
grammar 48–9, 115, 122, 123–4, 127
  modern 92, 93
  new 97, 99
  period of use 8, 9, 90
  rediscovery/interpretation 92, 96–103
  uses 58–60, 65
Hincks, Edward 121
historical texts
  administrative documents 76–7
  chronicles 74–5
  expedition records 78–9
  inscriptions 72–3
Horapollo 96, 97, 104
Hordjedef, Prince 80
Horemheb 14
Horus
  bird symbol 24, 32, 44
  cult of 99
  king as incarnation of 23
  name 23, 24, 27, 28, 31, 138
  sons of 65
  in stories 86, 87
  temple of 32, 63
Hu, temple pylon 112
human relationships 84–5

I
Ibada, Sheikh 47
Ikhernofret 68–9, 87
Imseti 65
inscriptions 58, 60, 72–3
Ipi, Vizier 85
Ipuwer, Lamentation of 80
Isis
  birth house of 99, 110
  bust of 102, 103

cult of 99
myth of Osiris 86, 97
temple of 90, 94, 112, 114, 118
Islam 97

J
Janelli, Cataldi 118
Julian Claudian dynasty 132

K
Kahun 85
Kalabsha 17
Kambyses 70
Kamose 70
Karnak
  Hypostyle Hall 62
  king-lists 74
  obelisks 98, 101, 105
  priests 31
  Red Chapel 81, 98
  temple of Amun-Re 31, 72
  temple of Khonsu 12
Khaefre 58, 65
Khasekhemwy 69
Khedeval Period 135
Kheruef, Steward 90
Khnumhetep 54, 84
Khonsu, temple 12
Khufu 80, 86
Kingdoms 132
kings
  alternative names 22, 128–9, 135
  chronology 132–5
  full list 130–2
  lists of 74, 113, 119, 122
  naming 22–9
Kingston Lacy 112, 118
Kircher, Athanasius 99–101, 102, 103, 104
Klaproth, Heinrich 118
Kleopatra III 115
Kleopatra VII 60
Kleopatra 110–11, 112
Kom Ombo 60, 88

L
labour force 13, 60, 76
Lacour, Pierre 109
Lahun 76
Lake Nasser 10, 17
language
  ancient Egypt 36
  development 36–7, 90, 92
  grammar 48–9, 122–4, 127
  Late Egyptian 36–7, 48, 51, 122, 138
Late Period 37, 90, 135
Lebanon 73
Lenoir, Alexandre 109
Lenormant, Charles 118
Le Page Renouf, Sir Peter
  see Renouf, Sir Peter Le Page

Lepsius, Karl Richard 92, 105, 119–21, 122, 124, 127
Lettre à M. Dacier, relative à l'alphabet des hieroglyphes phonétiques 113, 120
Lettre à M. le Professeur H. Rosellini sur l'Alphabet Hiéroglyphique 119, 124
lexicography 138
literature
  autobiographies 66–71
  chronicles 74–5
  chronology 58–9
  human relationships 84–5
  stories 86–7
  wisdom 80–1
love 84
Lower Egypt 14, 20, 30, 73
Luxor 36, 46, 62, 72, 98

M
Maat, goddess of truth 65
Macedonian kings
  chronology 135
  dynasty 90, 131
  language impact 37, 59, 90, 94
  names 26
magical texts 86, 88
Maharraqa, temple of 91
Mammisi 110
Manetho, priest 132
Marcel, Jean-Joseph 109
marriage 84–5
Maspero, Gaston 121
mastaba 64, 65
medical texts 88–9
Medinet Habu 70, 77
Meketre, Chancellor 87
Mekhu 68, 69
Memphis 13, 31, 93
Menkaure 27
Menou, General 106
Merenptah 19
Mesehti 71
Mesopotamia 17, 25, 121
Middle Egyptian 36, 48, 51, 122, 138
Middle Kingdom 59, 133
monarchy 135
Montjuhotpe IV 78, 79
morals 80, 87
mud brick buildings 11, 13
multiliterals 44, 118
mummies 88
museum collections 136–7
Mut, goddess 31

N
Nakhthorheb 97
names and titles
  alternate forms 22, 128–9, 135
  ancient Egyptians 31, 33

kings 21–9
officials 30–1
priests 31
queens 28, 29, 31
Napata 73
Napoleon Bonaparte 104, 106
Naqada I Period 10, 14
Naqada II Period 10, 14, 15
Naqada III Period 10, 14, 15, 133
Narmer Palette 20, 21
Nebty name 23, 27, 28, 138
Needham, John 102, 103
Nekhbet, goddess 23
Nelson, Horatio 106
Neolithic period 14
nesu-bity 24, 25, 30
New Kingdom
chronology 134
historical texts 59, 72
kings' names 23
language 36
world power 68, 72
Niankhkhnum 84
Niebuhr, Carsten 103
Nile, River 10–13
nomen 24, 26, 27, 28, 29, 138
nouns 48, 138
Nubia 91, 95, 96
Nubians 71, 73
numbers 25, 52–3

O
Obeliscus Pamphilius 102
obelisks
Bankes 105, 111, 112, 118
decipherment role 99–103
function 98
Hatshepsut 98, 105
Karnak 98, 101, 105
Philae 111, 112, 114, 118
Piazza Navona/Domitian 100, 101, 102, 103
Rome 99, 100, 102
offerings, list of 64
officials 30–1, 68, 70
Old Egyptian 36, 51, 122, 138
Old Kingdom 11, 36, 58, 133
ordinal 138
Osiris, god of the Dead
festival of 68–9
mortuary customs 45, 65
myth of 86, 87, 97, 99
Osorkon II 23, 26
Osorkon III 26
ostraka 45, 58, 76, 77
Ottoman Period 95, 135

P
Paganism 90
Palaeolithic period 14
Palermo Stone 74
Palestine 68, 70, 73, 79
Palin, Nils Gustaf 103, 109

papyrus
administrative documents 76
Book of the Dead 64–5
definition 61, 138
Edwin Smith surgical Papyrus 88
stories 86
uses 26, 58, 61
Westcar Papyrus 86
parents, of kings 29
Paser, Vizier 31
Pasherhorawesheb 64
Penzance, Egyptian House 93
Pepy I 68
Pepy II 68, 72
Persians 70, 135
pharaoh
see also kings
alternative names 135
derivation 32, 138
Philae
Christianity 90, 94
decrees 110
last hieroglyph 90, 92
obelisk 111, 112, 114, 118
temple of Isis 90, 94, 112, 114, 118
Philip Arrhidaios 26–7
philology 138
philosophy 80–1, 96, 97, 100, 101
Pius VI, Pope 103
Piye, Nubian king 73
Plotinus 96
Plutarch 97
poetry 72–3, 84
Polotsky, Hans Jakob 124
population 13
pottery
early evidence 10, 15
hieratic script 45, 58, 76, 77
Précis du système hiéroglyphique 115, 118
Predynastic Period 10, 14, 15, 20, 132
prenomen 24, 25–6, 27, 138
priests, titles 30, 31
princes, names 29
princesses, names 29
pronouns 48, 138
propaganda 72, 73, 75, 86
Protodynastic Period *see* Naqada III
Protosinaitic texts 79
Ptah, god 26, 27, 31
Ptolemaic Period
chronology 135
epithets 26
kings 132
language impact 37, 90, 94
literature 59
Ptolemy I 26
Ptolemy II 26–7
Ptolemy III 27, 110

Ptolemy V 110
Ptolemy VIII 115
Ptolemy XII 60, 110
Ptolemy, hieroglyph 107, 110, 112
Pyramid Texts 43, 58, 138
pyramids
building 11, 59, 60, 64, 65, 80
Dahshur 14, 60
Giza 11, 60, 65, 92, 111
Middle Ages view 97
modern hieroglyphs 92

Q
Qadesh, Battle of 73
Qasr Ibrim 96
Qebehsenuef 65
Qemau (Sihornedjhiryotef) 27
Qenhirkopshef, scribe 85
Qubbet el-Hawa 78
queens, naming 28, 29, 31

R
Raige, Remi 109
Rameses I 37
Rameses II
epithet 26
historical texts 62, 73, 75
temple 15, 34–5, 75, 95, 98
vizier 31
Rameses III 18, 29, 70, 76, 77
Rameses VI 19, 39, 62
Rameses IX 76
Ramose, Vizier 63
Rashid (Rosetta) 106, 107
Re, sun god
hieroglyph decipherment 113
king's names 23, 25, 26, 27, 56
ordinary names 31
in stories 86
temple of 98
rediscovery of hieroglyphs 96–103
Rekhmire, Vizier 72
religion
Christianity 46, 51, 90, 94–6, 97
Coptic 47
end of Paganism 90
hieratic script 47
Islam 97
last use of hieroglyphs 90
priests 31
rituals/festivals 63, 68–9
Renaissance period 97–9
Renouf, Sir Peter Le Page 119
Ricardi, Francesco 118
Roman period
chronology 135
decline of language 94
dynasty 94, 132

emperors' names 26, 27, 32
language development 37
literature 59
obelisks 98, 99, 100, 101, 102, 103
Rome, obelisks 99, 100, 102
Rosellini, Ippolito 121
Rosetta Stone 47, 90, 104–9, 111, 115

S
Sabni 68, 69
Sahure, temple 72
Saite Period 135
Salt, Henry 111, 112
Salvolini, François 115, 118, 121
Saqqara
king-lists 74
pyramids 59, 60
royal tombs 11
temple of Pepy II 72
tomb of Djehuty 69
tomb of Hemaka 61
tomb of Niankhkhnum and Khnumhetep 84
Scorpion, King 23
Seal-bearer of the King 30
Second Intermediate Period 36, 134
Seneferu 14
Sennefer 63
Senwosret I 28, 52, 69, 98
Senwosret III 56, 68, 73
serekh 21, 23, 24, 28, 138
Seth 23, 24, 63, 86, 87
Seth Peribsen 21
Sethe, Kurt 122
Sethy I
temple 75, 86, 99, 127, 127
tomb 44, 47, 111
Sethy II 76
Seyffarth, Gustavus 118–19
shen 24, 28
Shoshenq IV 28
Shu, god 29
Sinai 78
Sinuhe, story of 69, 86
Sisepdu 52
Siwa 90
Sixtus V 100
Sobek, god 33
Sobk and Haroueris, sanctuary of 60, 88
soldiers, autobiographies 70–1
songs 81, 84
sons, names 27, 29
spelling differences 128–9
sphinx 61
Spohn, Friedrich 118
St Nicholas, Tandeau de 109
Steindorff, Georg 122, 124
stela 24, 52, 53, 63, 64, 127
Stern, Ludwig 122

Stone Age 14
stone quarries 14, 78–9, 98, 100
stories 69, 86–7
Sudan 72, 73, 125
Syria 62, 68, 72, 73

T
Taharqa 72
Tanis 127
Tefnakhte 73
Tell Muqdam 13
temple domains 30–1
temples
  administrative documents 76
  conversion to churches 94, 95, 96
  early examples 14–15
  inscriptions 60, 62, 63, 64
  obelisks 98
tenses 48
Teti 98
Thebes
  administrative documents 76
  god of 27

God's Wife 31
  Nubian rule 73
  Ramesseum 15
  tomb of Amenemhab 70
  Wilkinson's work 115
Third Intermediate Period 37, 59, 134–5
Thoth 96, 99, 107, 113
Thutmose I 98
Thutmose III 26, 68, 69, 70, 72–3
Thutmose IV 26, 64, 101
titles 21–33, 138
Titus 27
Tiye, Queen 33
Tomb 100 15, 20
tombs
  see also funerary
  building stone 78
  inscriptions 60, 62, 63, 64, 69
  models 71, 87
trade 12, 17, 68, 72, 78, 88
transliteration 138
triliterals 44, 118, 138
Tunah el Gebel 96

Turin, Canon of Kings 122
Tutankhamun 19
Tuthmosis 107, 113, 115

U
U-j tomb 17
Udjahorresnet 70
Uhlemann, Max 119
Umm el-Qaab 15, 23, 25
Uni 68, 121
uniliteral 118, 138
Upper Egypt 14, 20, 30

V
Valerianus, Pierius 99
Valley of the Kings 15, 18–19, 64, 77, 111
Valley of the Queens 29
Verardi, Luigi 118
verbs 138
vernacular 138
vizier 30, 31, 63, 85
von Hammer Purgstall, Joseph 109
vowels 42

W
Wadi Hammamat 78, 79
Wadi el-Hol 79
Wadi Maghara 78
Wadi el-Sebua 95
Warburton, William 102, 104
Westcar Papyrus 86
Wilkinson, Sir John Gardner 115, 121
wisdom literature 80
women 32, 80, 84, 112
word signs 44
Wörterbuch der ägyptischen Sprache 123, 125
writing *see* demotic; greek; hieratic; hieroglyphs
writing media 58

Y
Young, Thomas 105, 106–10, 112

Z
Zoëga, Jørgen 103

PICTURE ACKNOWLEDGEMENTS

AMD Aidan Dodson
A Axiom Photographic Agency Ltd

BM: British Museum; CM: Cairo Museum; OMD: Oriental Museum Durham; RMS: Royal Museum of Scotland

t=top; *b*=bottom; *l*=left; *c*=centre; *r*= right

1 AMD/Louvre N3292; 2 James Morris/**A**; 3 James Morris/**A**; 5 James Morris/**A**; 6*t* James Morris/**A**, *c* James Morris/**A**, *b* AMD/Louvre E3023; 7*t* Chris Coe/**A**, *c* AMD/BM EA 24, *b* Chris Coe/**A**; 8–9 Chris Caldicott/**A**; 10*t* AMD, *bl* AMD/BM EA 58522, *bc* AMD/BM EA 36327, *br* AMD/Louvre E11255; 11*t* AMD, *bc* Peter Wilson/**A**, *br* Chris Caldicott/**A**; 12 AMD; 13*t* AMD, *b* AMD; 14*t* AMD, *b* AMD; 15 E. Simanor/**A**; 16 Chris Coe/**A**; 17*t* AMD, *b* AMD; 18–19 Chris Caldicott/**A**; 20*t* AMD/BM EA 32571, *b* AMD/CM; 21*t* AMD/Louvre E11255, *b* AMD/CM CG 14716; 23*t* AMD/Ashmolean Museum E 3632, *b* AMD; 24 AMD/Louvre E 11007; 25*t* AMD/BM EA 32650,55586, *b* AMD/Louvre AO29562; 26 AMD/CM JE 79195; 27 AMD/CM JE 40678; 28*t* James Morris/**A**, *c* James Morris/**A**; 29 James Morris/**A**; 30 AMD/Munich GL.WAF 38; 31 AMD/OMD N 511; 32*l* James Morris/**A**, *r* James Morris/**A**; 33*l* James Morris/**A**, *r* James Morris/**A**; 34–5 James Morris/**A** 36*t* AMD, *bl* AMD/Louvre E11007, *bc* AMD Louvre A 23; 37*t* James Morris/**A**, *b* AMD/Louvre E12982; 30 AMD; 40 AMD/Möller 1909–12; 41 AMD/Möller 1909–12; 42 AMD/RMS; 43 James Morris/**A**; 44 AMD/BM EA 5603; 45*tl* AMD/Louvre N328; 46 James Morris/**A**; 47*t* AMD/BM EA 884, *b* AMD/Louvre E12982; 48 AMD/Bristol H.4586; 49 AMD/BM EA 495; 50 James Morris/**A** ; 51 James Morris/**A**; 52*t* AMD/Louvre C 166; 52–3 James Morris/**A**; 54*t* AMD; 54–5 James Morris/**A**; 56 background AMD; 58 AMD/CM CG14; 59*t* James Morris/**A**, *bl* AMD/MFA 03.1631, *br* AMD/Manchester Museum; 60 AMD; 61*t* James Morris/**A**, *b* AMD/Louvre A23; 62*tl* Heidi Grassley/**A**, *tr* AMD, *b* AMD; 63*t* AMD, *b* AMD/CM JE 46993; 64*t* AMD, *b* AMD/BM 6666A; 65*t* James Morris/**A**,

b AMD/Louvre N3292; 66–7 AMD; 68 AMD/Luxor Museum J2; 69T AMD, *b* AMD; 70 James Morris/**A**; 71*t* James Morris/**A**, *b* James Morris/**A**; 72*t* James Morris/**A**, *b* AMD; 73*t* AMD, *b* AMD/CM CG 34010; 74*t* AMD/CM JE 65908, *bl* AMD/Turin N 1874, *br* AMD; 75*tl* James Morris/**A**, *br* AMD, *b* AMD; 76*t* AMD, *b* AMD; 77T James Morris/**A**, *c* AMD/RMS 1956.319, *b* AMD; 78*tl* AMD, *bl* AMD, *br* AMD/CM JE 57102; 79*t* AMD, *b* Sara Orel; 80*t* AMD/CM JE 36143; *b* AMD/Louvre E3023; 81 James Morris/**A**; 82–3 James Morris/**A**; 84 James Morris/**A**; 85*t* AMD/MMA, *b* AMD; 86 James Morris/**A**; 87 James H. Morris/**A**; 88 AMD/OMD; 89 James Morris/**A**; 90 Dyan Hilton; 91*t* AMD, *b* AMD; 92*t* AMD, *c* AMD, *b* E. Simanor/**A**; 93*tc* AMD, *r* AMD, *b* AMD; 94*c* AMD, *bl* AMD, *br* AMD/BM EA 1606; 95*t* AMD, *c* AMD, *bl* AMD/BM OA 10845, *br* Vanessa Fletcher; 96*t* Linda Pike, *b* James Morris/**A**; 97 *tl* AMD/BM EA 10, *tr* AMD, *b* AMD; 98*tl* E. Simanor/**A**, *tr* Chris Coe/**A**, *b* James Morris/**A**; 99*t* James Morris/**A**, *b* James Morris/**A**; 100*tl* AMD, *tc* AMD, *r* AMD; 101 AMD; 102 TL AMD, *tc* AMD; 103 *tl* Peter Clayton, *tr* AMD; 104*t* AMD, *bl* AMD, *br* AMD; 105*t* James Morris/**A**, *bl* AMD/BM EA 24, *br* AMD/Louvre; 106 AMD; 107*t* AMD/Commission des Monuments d'Egypte 1809–22 E.M.I. pl 81, *b* AMD/Commission des Monuments d'Egypte 1809–22 E.M.I. pl. 81; 108 AMD/BM EA 24; 109*t* AMD/Commission des Monuments d'Egypte 1809–22 A.V. pl. 52, *c* AMD Commission des Monuments d'Egypte 1809–22 A.V. pl. 53, *b* AMD/Commission des Monuments d'Egypte 1809–22 A.V. pl. 54; 110*t* AMD, *c* AMD/Louvre C 122, 111*t* AMD/*Illustrated London News*, 1874, *b* AMD/CM CG 22186; 112–3 James Morris/**A**; 114*t* AMD, *b* AMD/Louvre; 115 AMD/Louvre N3073; 116 Heidi Grassley/**A**; 117*t* AMD/Commission des Monuments d'Egypte 1809–22 A.I. pl. 17, *c* AMD, *b* AMD; 119*t* AMD, *b* AMD; 120 AMD; 121 AMD; 122 AMD/Budge 1893, facing p.1; 123 AMD; 125*tl* AMD, *br* AMD/Erman & Grapow 1926–31; 126 James Morris/**A**; 127*tl* AMD, *br* AMD, *b* AMD; 128–9 Chris Caldicott/**A**; 136 AMD; 137*tl* Chris Caldicott/**A**, *tr* James Morris/**A**, *b* AMD; 138 James Morris/**A**.

Jacket: Front *t* AMD; *b* James Morris/**A**; spine AMD; back James Morris/**A**.

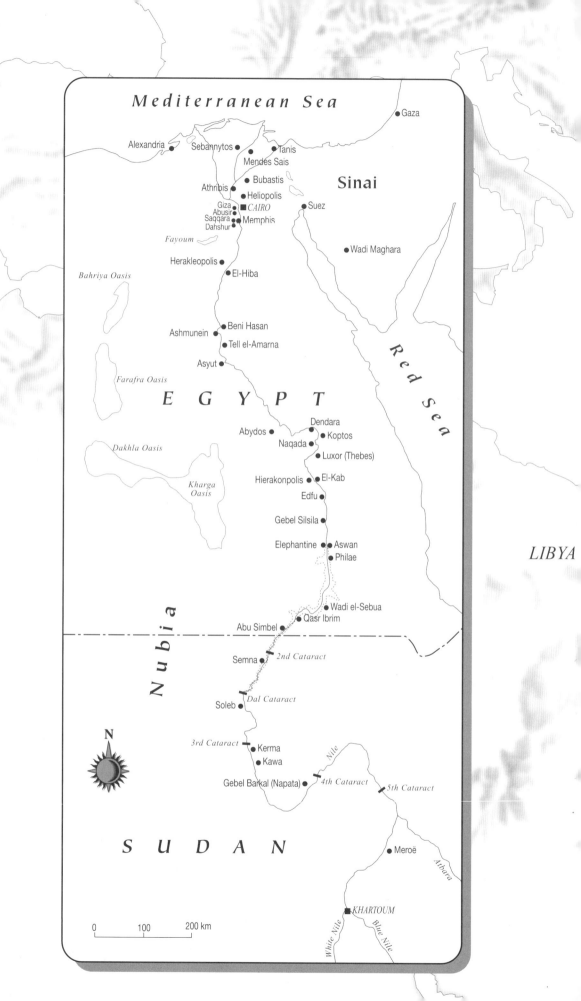